MARPLE'S
GRETCHEN HARRINGTON
TRAGEDY

MARPLE'S GRETCHEN HARRINGTON TRAGEDY

Kidnapping, Murder and Innocence
Lost in Suburban Philadelphia

MIKE MATHIS AND JOANNA FALCONE SULLIVAN

THE
History
PRESS

Published by The History Press
Charleston, SC
www.historypress.com

First published 2022

Manufactured in the United States

ISBN 9781467152587

Library of Congress Control Number: 2022943541

Notice: The information in this book is true and complete to the best of our knowledge. It is offered without guarantee on the part of the authors or The History Press. The authors and The History Press disclaim all liability in connection with the use of this book.

CONTENTS

PREFACE

We were ten years old when eight-year-old Gretchen Harrington was snatched off the street while walking to a Vacation Bible School class in August 1975. The crime forever changed our lives—so much so that, nearly fifty years later, we've never forgotten it.

Marple Township in the mid-1970s was a quiet suburban community with relatively little crime. Joanna's parents found it the perfect place to settle when they moved from south Philadelphia several months before the incident. Mike's parents decided to raise their family there when they moved from Buffalo, New York, in 1966 and lived temporarily in the Governor Sproul Apartments next to the Lawrence Park Shopping Center until they bought their house in Lawrence Park.

When Gretchen Harrington was kidnapped and murdered, life changed for us, our friends, our parents and all the adults in the community. We were no longer allowed to walk to our friends' houses or the swim club by ourselves. Our parents and our friends' parents watched over us more closely.

The crime made us more wary of strangers, which made us more cautious as we parented our own children. And we are perplexed that the crime is still unsolved nearly five decades after it happened.

We wrote this book as a tribute to Gretchen and to those of us whose childhoods were forever changed and whose adulthoods were shaped by her brutal murder.

Mike Mathis and Joanna Falcone Sullivan

ACKNOWLEDGEMENTS

We could not have completed this book without the assistance and support of Marple Township police chief Brandon Graeff.

I could not have embarked on or completed this project without Joanna Falcone Sullivan, my friend and classmate from Marple Newtown High School who shares a passion for storytelling.

I want to thank my wife, Beverly, for her love, patience and support; my children, Melissa, Michael and Anthony; and my grandchildren, Vincent, Evelyn, Violet and Lily.

—Mike Mathis

Special thanks to Ann (Harrington) Myers for letting me into her home and for sharing the memories of her beautiful sister Gretchen. I hope we were able to achieve Ann's goal of having Gretchen remembered as the sweet little girl she was.

I also want to acknowledge Marple police chief Brandon Graeff's cooperation in giving us access to the Harrington case file and for welcoming us into the station on several occasions. His passion to solve this murder highlighted Marple police's dedication to the case.

Of course, I couldn't have done this without my coauthor, Mike Mathis, a friend and Marple Newtown High School classmate who shares a passion for journalism.

And finally, a special thanks to my husband, Michael; son, Maxim; and my extended family—parents, Nick and Toni Falcone and Joan Sullivan; sisters, Angela Olden, Annamaria Concannon and Donna Steinfeldt—for their support and interest in this book. I appreciate your suggestions, edits and love.

We would also like to thank Nicholas Mancini for his graphic contributions and the Marple Township Police Department and Sharon Halota Bell for providing photographs.

—Joanna Falcone Sullivan

1

MISSING

August 15, 1975: The helicopter hovered over the woods near Lawrence Park Swim Club, cutting into the calm of a typically quiet August afternoon at the pool. Kids who were playing shuffleboard and volleyball and diving off the high dive rushed to see what was happening.

Parents at the sprawling swim club seemed unusually quiet, even tense. If they knew what was going on, they weren't saying.

Those kids would later learn that the helicopter was searching for Gretchen Harrington, an eight-year-old girl who disappeared on her way to Vacation Bible School at the Trinity Chapel, just a short walk from her home in the generally peaceful Philadelphia suburb of Marple Township, Pennsylvania, commonly known by the name of its primary post office, Broomall.

What remained of her body was found two months later about eight miles away from her home in a wooded area of Ridley Creek State Park. The crime has never been solved.

Gretchen's killing received little attention outside the Philadelphia area. It was a time before the internet and all-day cable news, but nearly fifty years later, her abduction and murder still haunt those who remember that day. The pain remains searing for her family members and close friends, who detail years of trauma after losing Gretchen. Yet there are many more strangers whose only connection to Gretchen was living in the same town who still think about the crime as a seminal moment in their lives—an event that signified a loss of innocence. Her death remains a topic of conversation in Facebook neighborhood groups, with current and former Broomall

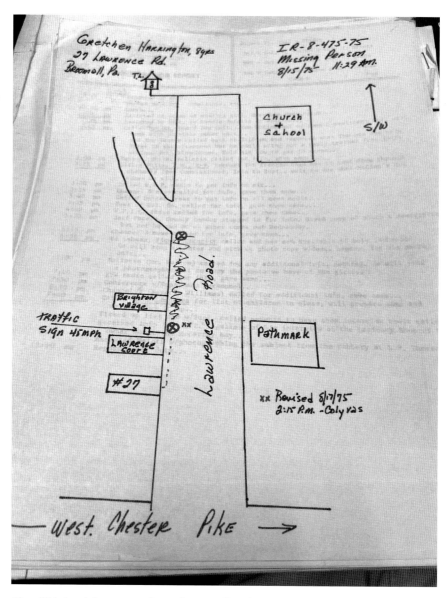

Above: This hand-drawn map shows the route Gretchen was believed to have taken from her home en route to the vacation bible school at Trinity Chapel Christian Reformed Church. *Marple Township Police Department*.

Opposite: Trinity Chapel Christian Reformed Church as it appeared on August 15, 1975. *Marple Township Police Department*.

residents offering eerily similar recollections of that day, the whirring helicopter playing a big part in their memories.

Gretchen's murder left an indelible impression on a generation of kids who, until then, thought their suburban world—just thirteen miles from the city line—was incredibly safe. They didn't grow up with electronics—video games were just starting to enter the picture. Cellphones wouldn't come along for more than a decade.

The kids of Broomall in 1975 played outside until well after dark. They rode bikes to their friends' homes without helmets. They walked to nearby stores and shopping centers in search of candy and soda. Parents often had no idea where their kids were, expecting them to only come in for dinner. It was a measure of freedom now considered idyllic in a time when kids aren't really allowed to roam anymore.

It's considered too dangerous today to wander, even on what are considered the safest of streets, until dark. Parents nowadays can track their children through an app on their cellphones and often ask them to check in when they're not with them.

That's why it's not surprising that this seemingly idealistic 1970s childhood is often thought of wistfully in a time when kids are glued to their phones, often eschewing the outdoors for a screen. Parents who let their children wander freely, even in the leafiest of suburbs, are labeled "free-range parents" and are looked down on by their more cautious peers. While the world today is considered far more dangerous for kids, it's a perception that isn't backed up by statistics.

The '70s were a tumultuous and crime-ridden era in the United States, when the nation's largest cities saw homicide rates soar. New York City was dubbed "Fear City" in the 1970s. The city's homicide rate more than doubled between 1960 and 1970. It was a trend fueled by economic uncertainty and social upheaval of the 1970s that made its way through cities across the nation.

David Schmid, an English professor at University of Buffalo, said there was a general lack of direction in the 1970s following the Vietnam War and the mass protests it triggered. Then the Watergate scandal created disillusionment among the populace. Inflation and a gas shortage literally added fuel to the fire. "There was that sense of being unsafe, of being that no one is looking out for us," Schmid said of the 1970s.

In Philadelphia, the number of homicides soared to 435 in 1975, more than doubling the 205 murders in 1965. Climbing street crime and the riots after Martin Luther King Jr.'s assassination in 1968 fueled an exodus of families from Philadelphia to suburbs like Broomall. The suburban building boom that started after World War II reached a frenzied level.

The '70s were also a time when a handful of the nation's most notorious serial killers began their killing sprees. The '70s brought Ted Bundy, John Wayne Gacy (the "Killer Clown"), California's Hillside Strangler and serial murderer Henry Lee Lucas, the latter even named a potential suspect in Gretchen Harrington's murder.

Whether Gretchen's murder was the work of a serial killer remains unknown, though police strongly believe it could have been the act of a known child rapist who died in jail. He was never charged with the crime. "Back then, serial killing was as common as it ever was," said Thomas Hargrove, a retired investigative journalist and founder of the nonprofit Murder Accountability Project. "Back in 1975, it didn't even have a name. Investigators with the FBI invented the serial killer name ten years later." Still, FBI statistics show that serial murder makes up less than 1 percent of killings in any year. But that fact hasn't made it any less frightening for generations who, since the late 1970s, have feared being killed by a lone madman.

Hargrove's Murder Accountability Project tracks the nation's unsolved homicides using FBI statistics and an algorithm that shows patterns or "clusters" of killings that could signify a serial killer was involved. Hargrove's interest in identifying serial killers came from his time spent as a reporter covering the Atlanta child murders, a series of twenty-four to thirty murders that rocked the southern city in the early 1980s. For that case, Wayne Bertram Williams is serving life imprisonment in Atlanta. He is believed to be responsible for twenty-four of the thirty child murders that took place between 1979 and 1981, but he was never tried for those crimes. Some doubts remain about whether he was truly the killer or made a convenient scapegoat by police. Williams remains in prison and has been denied parole repeatedly. Meanwhile, the case was reopened in 2019 so authorities could check DNA evidence in the child murders. Police have activated cases across the country to apply new DNA technology that can finally link suspects or even exonerate them in some cases.

Hargrove's database, which uses FBI crime statistics, offers stats for unsolved murders starting in 1976, so it doesn't include Gretchen Harrington's murder. Nor does it include several other high-profile murders of girls or young women that occurred in Delaware County, including the infamous Tinicum Swamp murders, in which the bodies of four girls were found in the waterways near Philadelphia International Airport. Those crimes were also never solved.

"During the Atlanta child murders, police were roundly criticized for not recognizing the patterns," Hargrove said. "Different detectives were assigned to different cases. It's a real problem. Criminologists think most series go unconnected for that reason."

Hargrove says the database of FBI crime statistics from the years following Gretchen's death do show an unusually high number of unsolved child murders—sixteen—that occurred in Delaware County between 1976 and 2020. He didn't spy a pattern of a serial killer, but he says that the high number and lack of clearance of the cases is unusual.

However, Hargrove said child murders have always been rare; few children are abducted and killed these days by strangers because parents don't let their kids out of their sight. "Back then, people weren't scared enough," he said. "Now, they're probably too scared."

Those who remember that fateful day in Broomall when Gretchen disappeared don't need data to disprove the notion that kids were safe then. Many kids never felt safe again. Their parents, in many cases, drew the reins tighter, no longer allowing their children to go on solo walks to the Lawrence Park Shopping Center or the Wawa convenience store.

Gretchen's older sister Harriet "Ann" Myers said her sister's death dispelled the romantic idea of a carefree childhood. Harriet, Gretchen and their oldest sister, Zoe, were among those kids who chased fireflies and played "capture the flag" and tag with the neighbor kids after the sun set. The three Harrington girls lived with their parents, Ena and the Reverend Harold Harrington at 27 Lawrence Road, a small brick Cape Cod–style home near the Broomall Reformed Presbyterian Church, the congregation their father presided over.

The girls' mother had come home with their infant sister, Jessyca, the day Gretchen disappeared. Until then, by many accounts, the family led a quiet and happy life surrounded by friends at church and in their tight-knit neighborhood. "In the summertime, we all played together," Myers recalled fondly, joking that she also spent a lot of time in church as the daughter of a minister. "Everybody was outdoors." Her fond memories unfortunately have been replaced with sinister ones. "People thought you didn't have to worry about the children," said Myers in an interview from her home in York, Pennsylvania. "They were wrong. They weren't safe—ever."

No, it wasn't safe—Marple Township police chief Brandon Graeff agreed. And though he said a prime suspect was not formally identified, he seemed determined that it will one day be solved for the sake of the Harrington family.

Gretchen's death remains one of Marple Township's few recorded murders to this day. Another is the unsolved case of Mary E. Hannig from 1972; she was shot in her driveway, allegedly by burglars. Then in 1985, there was Frank Forlini, who was gunned down and found in his truck in the parking lot of what was then the Kmart store on Reed Road, not far from where the Marple Township Police Station is currently located. Police believe Forlini's murder was not random.

Hannig's case, like Gretchen's, still baffles police. Graeff said the cases still come up in discussions during roll call and in other conversations among officers. "Gretchen is always at the top of that discussion," he said, adding, "Just about everybody is a parent and has that empathy."

The Hannig case has never been linked to Gretchen's, nor have any other nearby missing persons or murder cases.

Ann Myers said police did speculate that her sister's abduction and death may have been linked to that of another Delaware County, Pennsylvania girl. Fifteen-year-old Wendy Eaton, of nearby Media, went missing on May 17, 1975. Her body was never found. In May 2021, police classified Eaton's disappearance as a homicide. They began digging on a wooded property in Media, the county seat of Delaware County, Pennsylvania, after receiving new leads about the case. "I believe the state police have done a remarkable job of getting this case to the position where we're in right now," Delaware County district attorney Jack Stollsteimer told NBC Philadelphia about the digging in May 2021. "Where we think we can find some physical evidence on that property."

Police Chief Graeff wasn't familiar with the Eaton case, which is not unusual since he was only two at the time it occurred. But it also speaks to how Pennsylvania's township structure—small, individual governments with their own schools and police departments—wasn't conducive to information sharing technology in the 1970s. Landlines and the lack of internet didn't help. Yet Graeff is more than familiar with the Harrington case, despite having joined the Marple Police Department in 1997.

Most of the police officers who worked the Harrington case in the 1970s have since retired or died. It still haunts those detectives who never solved it. Some retired, expressing regret over the years that they couldn't find the little girl's killer.

Lieutenant Richard W. Mankin, who died in 2020, continued to work on the case for years before his retirement in 1993. Then a detective, he was the one of the first officers to arrive at the scene when her skeletal remains and clothing were found months after her disappearance. "It was really bad," he said in a July 29, 1977 interview with the *Delaware County Daily Times*. "It was something I'll never forget." Indeed, his son, Chuck, said his father never forgot. "Marple Township was surely not the place where a kidnapping would take place," said the younger Mankin, who was seven at the time of Gretchen's disappearance and turned eight—Gretchen's age—the following December. "It was a very quiet community of good people. I think the fact that it did and remained unsolved bothered my father much more than he let on."

Despite the many years that have passed, Gretchen's cold case remains open. The Pennsylvania State Police

Lieutenant Richard W. Mankin was the lead investigator in Gretchen Harrington's disappearance. Mankin was hired as a dispatcher for the Marple Township Police Department in August 1958. He became a police officer in September 1960, was promoted to detective in April 1966 and then to lieutenant in March 1977. He retired in April 1993 and died on June 22, 2020, at the age of eighty. He was a life member of the Marple Township Ambulance Corps. *Marple Township Police Department.*

refused to share files on the case or discuss the case, citing an ongoing investigation. A request to access those files via the Pennsylvania Right to Know Act was denied by state police.

At the Marple Police Station, the box containing police reports of the crime and other pertinent documents sat in Graeff's office when the authors of this book first visited the station. Graeff set aside hours for them to pore through the box, which was filled with documents pertaining to the crime. The contents of the box revealed details—some public, some not— about the Harrington case, interviews with potential witnesses and suspects and countless unsubstantiated tips about what happened that day. Some people even claimed they saw Gretchen after her disappearance, leading investigators to check out tips of possible little girls who looked like her. Nothing ever panned out. There's even an anonymous letter stored in a clear plastic bag that came from someone who wrote in years after the crime, raising the possibility that they knew the possible killer. The person never contacted police again.

Inside the manila folders, there were also numerous case files of reported indecent exposures, attempted abductions of children, other kidnappings or

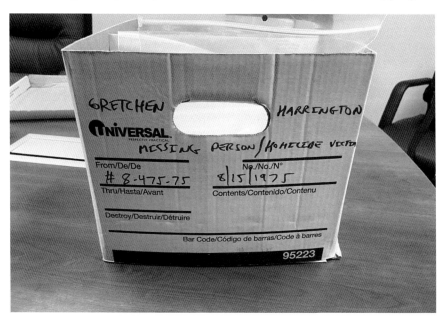

Reports, evidence and transcripts of interviews and old newspaper clippings about the Harrington case are stored in this single banker's box. Numerous detectives have pored over its contents in the years since Gretchen Harrington was killed, hoping a fresh set of eyes would help turn up a new lead that would solve the case. *Joanna Sullivan.*

murders of teens and young women both in nearby towns and out of state and a list of potential suspects in Gretchen's case and others. Many of the papers were yellowed and worn. In the '70s reports were either handwritten or typed. The cassette and reel-to-reel audio tapes in the box, which most likely include calls that were made to a tip line, are rendered useless by the advancement of technology. The police department has neither a cassette or reel-to-reel tape recorder with which to listen to them. In the box, there's even an old map of Ridley Creek State Park with the spot where Gretchen's body was found marked in ink. The evidence box also includes the smiling mugshot of a man whom some retired Marple detectives who worked the case are convinced was Gretchen's killer. The man was jailed for the rape of another young girl and was in the vicinity of Gretchen's home and church the day she disappeared.

The mystery of Gretchen's disappearance and death endures, despite decades of police work. Only the hope of modern technology and perhaps the usage of DNA testing might finally help solve the crime. DNA technology is increasingly being used to link suspects to long-cold cases. The proliferation of genealogy testing is aiding police as well. And Marple police officers do wonder whether such technology could be deployed in this case.

Until the case is solved, Gretchen's family and those who knew her will continue to wonder who infiltrated their world nearly fifty years ago and shattered any illusions they had of peace and well-being for the rest of their lives. "This isn't closed. It's a cold case," Graeff said of the investigation. "It's not closed by any means."

Graeff said that, once again, a young detective has taken on the Harrington case. This time around, it's Detective Nick Coffin, who started reviewing the files for the first time, optimistic that he might catch something that was missed before.

If Coffin doesn't solve it, Graeff is assured that yet another detective will pick up the case at another time. The case "stays alive," he added, noting that some police officers will never give up on a case. "It sounds corny, but there is certainly a desire for justice if not for the family but for Gretchen," Graeff said. "There's that sense of carrying the torch for the victim—for her."

2

"SHE'S GONE. I KNOW SHE'S GONE."

Ann Myers thinks she was the first to notice Gretchen was missing. The rest of the day her younger sister disappeared is a blur. That hasn't stopped her from reliving the day "over and over" in her mind through the years. She pauses as she tries to again remember what her ten-year-old self was thinking and feeling. "It was just really chaotic. I was trying not to cry. There were reporters at the door."

But Myers's most distinct memory is of how her parents irrevocably changed that day. "It seemed like my dad was always on the phone," she said. "My mom was not herself. Nobody was themselves."

Myers said she doesn't know what's real or what isn't about August 15, 1975. For a while, the entire family seemed to have the same story, making her wonder whether her memories of that day were corrupted by pictures, news stories and time. The family never really discussed the day in detail over the years. "My parents either forgot or weren't willing to discuss it," Myers added.

There are numerous accounts with varying details from news reports, police reports and witness recollections about what happened when Gretchen Harrington disappeared. Police say Gretchen left her home near the Lawrence Park neighborhood of Marple Township around 9:20 a.m. to attend the last day of the weeklong Vacation Bible School at the Trinity Chapel, a Christian Reformed church at 144 Lawrence Road. The church was about a half-mile from her home, up the steep hill of Lawrence Road, a busy road dotted with houses, apartment buildings, churches and, at the time, a Pathmark supermarket.

Gretchen's sisters, Ann and Zoe, had walked with her the other days that week. The girls would walk up the hill a few blocks to a traffic light and then cross busy Lawrence Road to the Bible school, according to state police in news reports. But on the day she disappeared, Gretchen was alone. Her father watched her leave the house and walk up the hill in her blue sneakers.

Reverend Harrington and the rest of the family's routine was disrupted that day. Ena Harrington had just come home with their newborn daughter, Jessyca. "The day my wife came home from Bryn Mawr Hospital, Gretchen was murdered," Reverend Harrington would later tell a newspaper reporter.

There are differing versions of the exact time when people realized Gretchen was missing. Reverend Harrington reported that his daughter was missing at 11:29 a.m., according to a Marple police incident report filed that day. A news report said that Reverend Harrington first realized Gretchen was missing "when several of her friends came to the front door of the church's manse without her at about 1:01 p.m. He checked the classes and was unable to locate her," the *News of Delaware County* reported.

Reverend David Zandstra, the pastor of Trinity Chapel, recalled he notified police that Gretchen was missing after one of the Bible school teachers told him she was not in class. The first hour of the Bible school was conducted at Trinity Chapel before the kids, numbering about sixty and of various ages, were sent to the Reformed Presbyterian church nearby. "I was running a Volkswagen bus with a certain amount of children to bring them to the church building, and when I got there, I think one of the teachers from Gretchen's class asked me if I had seen Gretchen," Reverend Zandstra said in a recent interview. "She said, 'I thought Gretchen might be with you,' and I said no. She said, 'She's not here.'" Reverend Zandstra continued, "Either I called, or I went to Pastor Harrington's house, and they confirmed that she had left to walk up the street. And I said she's not here. I must have at that point called the police."

Margie Zandstra, the Trinity Chapel minister's wife, said she remembered Reverend Harrington coming up to the church and saying, "She's gone. I know she's gone." She continued, "He said, 'I usually watch her walk up the street, but for that day, I only watched her a little bit and then I went into the house.'"

Lieutenant Richard Mankin said in a 1988 interview that the killer lured Gretchen to a vehicle and grabbed her between 9:20 a.m. and 9:30 a.m. on the east side of Lawrence Road between the Lawrence Court Apartments and Brighton Village Apartments. He said she was last seen by the mother of another Bible school student driving by who had dropped off her child.

Lawrence Road looking north toward Sproul Road on August 15, 1975. *Marple Township Police Department.*

This portion of Lawrence Road runs parallel to the four-lane section of the highway from which Gretchen was snatched. *Mike Mathis.*

Lawrence Road in front of St. Pius X School. Trinity Chapel can be seen beyond the school at the traffic signal. *Marple Township Police Department.*

Mankin told reporter John Roman that the traffic was light on the typically busy Lawrence Road. The nearby St. Pius X School, a Catholic institution affiliated with the St. Pius X Church, was closed for the summer.

Mankin said police were never able to link reports of a white car and a green pickup truck that were seen in the area.

"She wouldn't voluntarily get into a car with a stranger," Mankin said in the interview.

Marple police detective Fred Blanck told the *News of Delaware County* in an August 21, 1975 story that a woman who lived between the Harringtons' home and the church told Marple police that she saw Gretchen walk past her home about five minutes after she left for the church.

Marple Township police believed Gretchen was abducted about one hundred yards from her home during her half-mile walk to the Bible school. Police speculated that "Gretchen was taken by someone she thought she knew that sunny August 15," the *Delaware County Daily Times* reported. The news story quoted police saying that Gretchen approached a vehicle on Lawrence Road because "she thought the driver looked familiar."

On August 17, Sharon Smith, a woman who lived on Broomall's Hampshire Drive, reported to police that while she was going to work on August 15 and waiting for the traffic light to change at Sussex Boulevard and Lawrence Road, she saw the occupant of a car stop and talk to a young girl. The woman said she made the light and turned to go down the hill of Lawrence Road and didn't see whether the girl got into the car or not, according to a police report.

Numerous reports mentioned a pickup truck that was seen stopped on Lawrence Road where Gretchen was walking. Police said the pickup was described as "dark green with a missing tailgate." Smith told police the car was either a green station wagon or a Cadillac with a light top and dark bottom. The pickup was described by witnesses as an "older model, medium dark green pickup truck, no tailgate, fenders protrude from side of body rather than being straight-sided." The truck had Pennsylvania tags, a dent on the left rear fender, a plywood sheet on the bed and "some sort of yellow pump-like article with aluminum handles in the back," according to the report. The report also said it had no rack or sideboards.

The other car was described as an "older model, white four-door car with the paint dull and in poor condition, 'boxy' and hard to tell front from back at a distance." A police report said the car's hood ornament "recessed into the hood" and that there was possibly a vent window in the rear door.

In August, after Gretchen's body was found, police surmised that the white vehicle may have been disposed of after the crime.

A witness connected at least one white male to the white car. He was described in a police report as being between sixteen and twenty-three years of age; approximately five feet, seven inches tall; medium build; and with collar-length hair square across the back. The subject was wearing shorts, a tank-type shirt and sneakers, the report said.

In an October 1975 memo, Marple police said the information on the potential suspects was confidential and for "police information only."

Then on December 8, 1975, an anonymous phone call came into *Delaware County Daily Times* city editor Don Beideman that specifically named the make and model of the white car. A woman, described as "white, age fifty to sixty upwards, sober and rational," said she witnessed the abduction of Gretchen. She told Beideman that two people forced the little girl into a white Ford car with the Pennsylvania tags of 65K-907. Beideman asked why she didn't report this sooner, according to a Pennsylvania State Police report. The woman said she did not want to become "involved with the police in any way" and that that was why she called the newspaper to pass on the

The Marple Township Police Station as it appeared in the late 1960s. *Sharon Halota Bell.*

information. She mentioned that Christmas was coming and that the Harrington case "bothers her." She said she wanted to clear the air. When asked to provide some method of contacting her again, the woman refused and hung up.

Speculation about that woman's call, the white car, the green—in some cases described as blue—pickup and men seen near the crime scene continues to this day.

Mrs. Zandstra remembered the hopeful speculation that surrounded the little girl's disappearance. She said some believed that Gretchen went to a store to buy her new baby sister a gift, but Mrs. Harrington said such a move would have been out of character for her. "I don't think she would either," Mrs. Zandstra said. "She was not a precocious child at all. She wouldn't do anything unusual."

Kristi Zandstra Brierton, Margie Zandstra's daughter and a close friend of Gretchen's, said those panicked moments at Bible school are like "pictures in her head." "I remember a sense of panic in the air," Zandstra Brierton recalled. "My parents looked very scared. There were other adults around. I sensed this urgency, but I didn't understand the magnitude of them thinking she was gone gone." She recalled someone, possibly a police officer, asking her whether Gretchen would run away or if she was jealous of her new sister. That theory about Gretchen, raised by a young classmate of the missing girl, was disputed by Reverend Harrington, police said in a report. "At the time, I really think I lived under the assumption that she would come back," Zandstra Brierton said. "I did not think in any way my friend is gone or is dead. I thought I don't know where she is, but eventually, she's coming back."

Reverend Zandstra's call launched search efforts by Marple and nearby Haverford township police and firefighters and soon after by three hundred volunteers from the community. They combed the streets, nearby wooded areas and a local creek. Darby Creek, a tributary of the Delaware River, flows parallel to Lawrence Road, where Gretchen was last seen. Gretchen's home on the Broomall Reformed Presbyterian Church property sat right up against the creek.

"It was almost to me like I was looking for my sister," said Kevin McMenamin, a junior firefighter with the Broomall Fire Company. His

Investigators searched this section of Darby Creek behind the Broomall Reformed Presbyterian Church and parsonage after Gretchen disappeared. *Mike Mathis.*

sister was nine years old at the time, a year older than Gretchen. "That was all I kept thinking, because they were the same age," he said. "I wasn't a thirty-year-old guy. I was a kid, and I was scared to death for that kid."

McMenamin was among those who was tapped to help search for the missing girl in the woods across Lawrence Road from her home, specifically the woods next to Langford Road in the area of the nearby Lawrence Park Swim Club. McMenamin recalled that he participated in two searches of the area over that weekend. He said those who participated in the search for Gretchen were limited to firefighters and police from Marple and adjacent Haverford and Newtown Townships. "I remember going down the Lawrence Road hill, where the Pathmark (supermarket) was," McMenamin remembered. "I remember the shock of it all. It was the '70s, and that kind of stuff didn't happen."

The Pathmark store, and its employees were part of the police investigation, according to documents found in Marple police's case file. Police looked at the backgrounds of those who worked there, mostly people from outside the Broomall community.

McMenamin recalled, "After the search, we went back to the fire company; the police briefed us on what they found, and I don't remember them saying that they found anything at all, any evidence, picked up anything that would be valuable." McMenamin remembered that after the search by firefighters and police failed to turn up anything, the search party was widened to include dozens of men who had children of Gretchen's age. "That was after they took the police tape away," McMenamin said. "For the initial searches, they weren't letting civilians near it."

Arthur Candenquist, the secretary of the Broomall Fire Company, later wrote a letter thanking the firefighters and civilians who assisted in what proved to be a futile search. "The going was rough," he wrote in his open letter. "Most of the areas searched are a hopeless jungle of vines and underbrush, infested with mosquitoes. The weather was drizzling and humid. Not once did anyone complain nor shirk their responsibility once they committed themselves to helping a family most of us did not know personally." Candenquist pointed out that many of the volunteers wanted to do more than just stand by and watch the firefighters and police at work. "In a time when most Americans choose not to be involved with their neighbors, it was certainly gratifying to see the group which turned out," he wrote.

Dawn Keiser Watson, a close friend of Gretchen's who was also eight at the time, remembered parents from the nearby homes and apartments dividing into groups. Some fanned out into the woods. Others held hands and waded through the creek in search of any signs of the missing girl.

"We all began searching the neighborhood, as I did not live far from her home," said Jim Christaldi, a neighbor from Lawrence Park, remembered. "I knew the woods that were connected to her backyard like the back of my hand, having spent just about every waking hour in them as a child." He continued, "We searched high and low through those woods and everywhere else we could think. We didn't think to go up and search Ridley Creek State Park though. This was something quite new to us back then. Children did not disappear and end up molested and murdered. It was a very sad time for us. It seemed like it was the beginning of a horrible trend."

A state police helicopter dispatched from the city of Reading, Pennsylvania, circled above in search of the missing girl. Searchers were given the description of Gretchen: three feet, six inches tall; weighing fifty to sixty pounds, with light brown hair and blue eyes. She was wearing a blue and white short-sleeved striped shirt, dark blue shorts and blue sneakers "with other colors on the toes," according to a story in the *News of Delaware County*.

Above: Marple Township police superintendent Daniel Hennessey (*sitting center*) headed the department at the time of Gretchen Harrington's disappearance. He is flanked by Lieutenant Richard W. Mankin (*left*) and Lieutenant Frank Dunn (*right*). *Marple Township Police Department.*

Opposite: Marple Township police designed this poster, which was distributed widely in the days after Gretchen Harrington's disappearance. *Marple Township Police Department.*

"No one would allow us to go anywhere—everyone was afraid," Keiser Watson recalled, echoing many others' recollections of hearing the incessant whir from up above. "I just remember the helicopter," Keiser Watson said. "I remember all the people in the parking lot. I remember it being night, everybody calling her name."

Philadelphia police detectives and K-9 bloodhound units searched the woods between Langford and Lawrence Roads in Marple. But the dogs were called off the next day because the rain had lessened the chance of them picking up a human scent, the *News of Delaware County* reported.

"I remember my mom saying Gretchen was missing and asked whether she had seen her," Keiser Watson said. "Her dad had been at bottom of the hill and watched her go [to Bible school]. She didn't make it."

None of the sightings made sense to the Harringtons. In a newspaper story, Ena Harrington was quoted as saying she raised her daughters "to be careful." She said they were even cautious of the mailman, who they saw

MISSING PERSON

RACE: WHITE

SEX: FEMALE

AGE: 8 (DOB 6/13/67)

HEIGHT: 4 Ft. 6 In. (App.)

WEIGHT: 60 LBS (App.)

HAIR: LIGHT BROWN, SHOULDER LENGTH.

EYES: BLUE

COMPLEXION: FAIR

NOTE: MISSING TOOTH TOP RIGHT SIDE. HAS HAD NO DENTAL WORK DONE, HAS HAD NO CAVITIES.

REFER: OUR CASE NO. 250-453 UNISCOPE - HAV 324, AUG. 16, 1975

GRETCHEN HARRINGTON

SUBJECT WALKED AWAY FROM HER HOME AT 27 LAWRENCE ROAD, BROOMALL, DELAWARE COUNTY, PENNSYLVANIA AT APPROXIMATELY 9:20 A.M. ON FRIDAY, AUGUST 15, 1975 TO WALK SOUTHWESTERLY ON LAWRENCE ROAD TO THE TRINITY CHAPEL BIBLE SCHOOL APPROXIMATELY ONE-THIRD OF A MILE AWAY. WAS LAST KNOWN TO BE SEEN APPROXIMATELY ONE-TENTH OF A MILE FROM HOME IN THAT DIRECTION. SHE WAS WEARING HER HAIR IN "PIG TAILS". WORE A BLUE & WHITE STRIPED, SLEEVELESS TOP, MEDIUM BLUE SHORTS WITH ZIPPER AND SNAP CLOSURE AND TWO FRONT POCKETS, BLUE SNEAKERS WITH MULTI-COLOR TOES.

ANY INFORMATION NOTIFY; DETECTIVE BUREAU

MARPLE TWP. POLICE DEPARTMENT - 215-356-1500

SPRINGFIELD & SPROUL RDS.   BROOMALL,PA.   19008

on a regular basis. "I will never understand why she went with a stranger," Ena Harrington said in the story. "[Police] said a pedophile had maybe been watching the girls all week."

Keiser Watson also recalled being told that about the woman who had witnessed something from her home. "She never came forward again," she said. "She had seen something—never came forward again."

But no one else near the property caught even a glimpse of what happened that morning. The day proved to be long and trying as the search dragged on.

"We continued on with the Bible school that morning but with heavy hearts," Mrs. Zandstra said. "We went down [to the Harringtons' house] later in the day, about dinner time, and I took them some dinner, and she had not appeared by that time, so we were pretty sure that something bad happened." Mrs. Zandstra said she visited Ena and Reverend Harrington the day Gretchen disappeared and found the little girl's mother, who had just come home with her baby, almost resigned to a bad outcome. "She wasn't crying," she said. "She was just kind of accepting the fact that [Gretchen] was gone. I don't know whether she was just putting on a brave face. I think she was in shock. I think she just was in disbelief."

The formal search was called off the Sunday after Gretchen's Friday disappearance. Chief Hennessey assured the community that the department "would devote all our resources" to finding Gretchen. "But," he told the *News of Delaware County*, "We haven't got a clue." He remarked that the trail had gone cold quickly despite many tips and an exhaustive search. "Since then, we haven't been able to find so much as a trace of her," Chief Daniel Hennessey told reporter Erma Shaver.

Gretchen's second grade photograph was used on posters that were handed out to passing motorists the Monday after her disappearance. The flier showed a smiling Gretchen, her long brown hair pulled back with a barrette and a tooth missing on the right side of her mouth. Myers said the family never received the photograph back. It remains a vacant spot in a photograph album that holds Gretchen's kindergarten and first-grade photographs, pictures of baby Jessyca and shots of a family vacation in Canada.

The fliers and news coverage prompted many tips and even false sightings of little girls who fit Gretchen's description.

The days following Gretchen's disappearance were marked with fear that something horrible happened to her. Margie Zandstra recalled a feeling of dread. "I do remember not sleeping that night, and it was pouring rain, and I thought this poor child is out there somewhere in the rain and cold," Mrs. Zandstra said.

3

WHO WAS GRETCHEN HARRINGTON?

Ann Myers thinks of her family's timeline as being split: "before" and "after" Gretchen's death. "We all changed. It changed our family," she said. "Our dynamics are kind of messed up."
Ena Harrington brought her baby daughter, Jessyca, home the day Gretchen was abducted. What should have been a period of joy, welcoming a new baby, turned into a harrowing time for the family. For Myers, who was then ten, and Zoe, who was eleven, the trauma has lasted for decades. According to Myers, the entire family was irrevocably broken after her younger sister's murder. Myers said she wasn't surprised when her family stopped talking publicly or even privately about losing Gretchen.

"It has been hard for her in a completely different way," Myers said of her sister Jessyca. "She didn't know the parents we knew. It must have been confusing for her. She knew a 'Humpty Dumpty' family." Myers said she feels bad that Jessyca, as a child, didn't know the parents that she and her other sisters experienced. "My parents tried," she added. "Their heart wasn't in it."

Myers remembers life was good before tragedy befell her family. "My fondest memories are of school," she said. The three Harrington girls attended Delaware County Christian School, a well-regarded K–12 private school in nearby Newtown Square, Pennsylvania. She also remembers a lot of evening church. "When you're a minister's daughter, you go to church all the time," she said with a laugh.

Ann Myers discusses how the kidnapping and murder of her sister affected her life and the lives of her family members during an interview in her home in York, Pennsylvania, in 2021. *Joanna Sullivan*.

The family's "before" life revolved around the church, which is not unusual for the family of a preacher. By all accounts—and also as evidenced in the interviews the church pastor gave after Gretchen's death—Reverend Harrington's figure loomed large in the family, church and community. Reverend Harrington, who died on November 16, 2021, was remembered in an obituary for being "happiest when fully engaging his curious mind, leading to many a spirited dinner conversation."

Reverend Harrington, a native of Hetherton, Michigan, found his way into religious life by a circuitous route. He served in the U.S. Navy after graduating from high school in 1946. He attended Geneva College in Beaver Falls, Pennsylvania, to pursue a degree in engineering. He ended up graduating in 1949 with an arts degree. He later attended seminary school and was ordained as a minister in 1951. His obituary said he studied for several years at the University of Edinburgh and spent time traveling through Europe via bike and motorcycle.

Reverend Harrington's ministerial career began in September 1954, when he led several congregations of the Reformed Presbyterian Church

Delaware County Christian School on Malin Road in Newtown Township. Gretchen Harrington had finished the second grade at the school and was preparing to enter the third grade when she disappeared. *Author's Collection.*

of North America. Harrington was ordained and installed as the pastor of the New Castle, Pennsylvania congregation in 1954. After serving with the New Castle congregation for seven years, he worked in Arizona with the church's security commission from 1961 to 1964. It was during this time that he married Ena Fay Cover on March 16, 1962. They were married for fifty-nine years at the time of his death. The couple moved to Lake Reno, Minnesota, when Harrington took over a congregation there until 1967. His work then took him back to New Castle. The church's history says, "A call was made to Reverend Harrington. Accepting, he was installed as pastor of the Broomall congregation June 19, 1968."

The church's history talks about the "troubled times" of the late 1960s and how Reverend Harrington provided solid leadership during this tumultuous era:

> *The civil rights movement continued, and the war in Vietnam was sapping the resolve of the country. Mass antiwar demonstrations and sit-ins were becoming common, often resulting in violence. It seemed as though the nation was self-destructing before our very eyes. Sexual immorality became the ultimate weapon in the arsenal of the antiestablishment "hippie" revolution.*
>
> *Reverend Harrington provided able leadership for the flock under his care throughout the trials of the sixties. There was an ongoing effort to minister in a special way to the young members of the congregation—knowing what temptations they faced.*

The Harringtons' life in Pennsylvania began in the middle of Reverend Harrington's long religious career. The family moved to Broomall when Myers was three and a half years old, as her father was to take over as pastor of Broomall Reformed Presbyterian Church. "For two years, my congregation tried calling one 'star' after another. None were interested in our small, aging

The Broomall Reformed Presbyterian Church as it appeared in 2021. *Mike Mathis.*

The parsonage at the Broomall Reformed Presbyterian Church, where the Harrington family lived at the time of Gretchen's disappearance. *Mike Mathis.*

planet," wrote Reverend Bill Edgar in Reverend Harrington's obituary in 2021. "So, Broomall called Harold. He was installed on June 19, 1968."

The Broomall Church, founded in Philadelphia in 1798, is a congregation of the Reformed Presbyterian Church of North America, a sector of the Presbyterian Church with a strong belief in and practice of the Bible's teachings. The church's history goes back to the Covenanters of Scotland, a group that the church says defied the king and refused to become part of the Church of Scotland. Members of Covenanters migrated by the thousands to America in the 1700s to avoid persecution by the national church.

Along with strong praise for Reverend Harrington and his family, the church's history also chronicles Gretchen's abduction and murder. It talks of how the family's faith helped them endure, a sentiment echoed by Ena and Reverend Harrington in interviews at the time. "Words can never convey what the Harringtons endured," the church's history said. "They have indeed endured, a token of God's graciousness in the midst of great sorrow. Even through this grief, Reverend Harrington has continued to serve the Lord in the preaching of his word."

Edgar addressed Gretchen's death in Reverend Harrington's obituary:

> *The tragedy that would send most men out of the pastorate, at least for a time, saw Reverend Harrington resolutely where he belonged, preaching salvation through Christ.…The Lord's Day after Gretchen disappeared, Reverend Harrington preached to a congregation that sang Psalms to God with tears streaming down their faces. He never hid how he missed Gretchen, and we were welcome to talk about her.*

Reverend Harrington continued to lead the congregation in Broomall until 1980 and even returned over the years when the congregation's pastor was away.

The former theology professor was known for his powerful sermons—probably none as forceful as the one he gave six days after his daughter's body was found. "Gretchen, with her simple faith in Christ, is free," the *Philadelphia Bulletin* reported he said from the pulpit. "But her murderer is in terrible bondage. We could wish that Christ would set him free as well." Harrington made these statements during a forty-minute sermon at an 11:00 a.m. Sunday service. He said that "the forces of evil" may have intended the murder to "somehow shut up [his] preaching of the Gospel. "And so, while I would rather be somewhere else today, I determined that I would come here and preach," he said.

Harrington said he wrote the majority of the sermon, based on Acts 2 of the New Testament, the day before Gretchen was found. He added the references to her a few days before he delivered it, the *Philadelphia Bulletin* reported. His harsh words about society seemed to echo his earlier sentiments about the decline of society during the turbulent 1960s. This time, he cited Gretchen's and other local girls' deaths. He described today's society as "a moral cesspool." He said during the sermon, "The world is filled with unspeakable evil because of the wickedness of the human who knows the truth but will not accept it."

Reverend Harrington led the Broomall church for five years after his daughter's death. Myers now wonders why they stayed so long. She thinks her parents didn't want to leave while the investigation was still ongoing.

Not surprisingly, Myers doesn't wax nostalgic about her life in Broomall. She remembered that a Pathmark supermarket was being built and that the state was getting ready to build the Blue Route, a controversial highway that was more than a decade in the making. Construction began on the 132.1-mile highway, officially Route 476, in 1970. It would eventually open in 1991, linking Interstate 95 to the Pennsylvania Turnpike. Its construction changed the Harringtons' neighborhood and much of Philadelphia's western suburbs. Myers especially remembered the noise from the construction. Nearby Lawrence Road and West Chester Pike, both major thoroughfares in Marple Township, were already busy roads, with horns honking and sirens blaring as they headed to nearby Haverford Hospital on West Chester Pike.

Myers does have fond memories of walking down to the old Gentile's market, a family-run business known for its fresh produce. "We would walk down there and get vegetables," she said. "I remember that place."

Myers's father drove a Corvair, a vehicle that led to a lifelong obsession and an extensive collection of the classic cars. (His obituary said, "The neighborhood loved when he had nineteen!") Her mother worked in the nearby Lawrence Park Industrial Center.

Myers remembered being happy. She remembered her sister Gretchen as an even happier child, innocent and uncomplicated. "She was sensitive. She liked people," Myers said. "She didn't have a mean streak in her body at all. She was a nice person." Myers described her sister Gretchen as "a nice little girl who loved the TV show *Gunsmoke* and couldn't match her clothes." "She'd wear stripes with plaid," she said. "She didn't care."

And Myers remembered that Gretchen liked board games and card games. "Gretchen wouldn't be left behind," she said, adding the little girl

Gretchen Harrington as a kindergartner. *Ann Myers.*

insisted on playing games with her older sisters. "She didn't want to be left out." The Harrington girls played *Monopoly*, *Sorry!* and *Chutes and Ladders*. "*Chutes and Ladders* was Gretchen's favorite," she recalled. "It's just based on chance. You can win. It's not skill."

Kristi Zandstra Brierton called Gretchen "one of those just easygoing kids." She and Gretchen met through their fathers, both ministers, and attended Delaware County Christian School together; they became close friends. "We never fought," Zandstra Brierton said. "We just had fun together." She continued, "We played together for as long as I can remember. We both had big yards with the parsonage, the church and the church grounds, and so we did a lot of playing outside—you know, swings, climbing trees, things like that." Zandstra Brierton said that, at school, "Gretchen was friends with everybody, and she was happy to play with anybody."

Dawn Keiser Watson was one of those playmates. Gretchen attended Keiser Watson's eighth birthday on August 14, the day before she was abducted. Keiser Watson's family lived in the apartment near the Harringtons' house. "She always had a dress on," Dawn added. "She was always dressed really nice. She was shy. But she was fun." Dawn continued, "She was always smiling. We used to play jump-rope, climb trees all the time." Dawn's sister Jodi Keiser Gerrity said, "I just remember her being such a sweet friend. My mom would always say how shy she was."

Gretchen's playmates, now grown women with children of their own, have fond memories of their playmate's parents as well. Zandstra Brierton spoke highly of Ena Harrington, recalling her as a "very peaceful pastor's wife type." "Her mom always seemed like such a like a gentle soul to me," Zandstra Brierton said of Ena Harrington. "She never yelled. She was very calm about everything." Keiser Gerrity recalled, "They were a very close-knit family."

Jim Christaldi delivered the newspaper to the Harrington family and described Gretchen and her sisters as "a very cute little family." "I just remember going to the door to get paid as the paper boy when I had been younger and seen all the kids and the parents," he said. "They seemed like a really nice family, and I just couldn't begin to fathom their loss. I remember being desperate to try to find this little girl."

Above: Trinity Chapel Christian Reformed Church as it appeared in 2021. *Mike Mathis*.

Left: Gretchen Harrington as a first grader. She was preparing to enter the third grade when she disappeared. *Ann Myers*.

Ena and Reverend Harrington stopped talking publicly about their murdered daughter years ago. They gave some interviews over the years but eventually just continued to live their lives. Ann Myers was the only Harrington family member, aside from Myers's daughter Sarah Myers, who responded to a request to talk about that terrible day and its aftermath.

Interviews in the media with Reverend Harrington and Ena Harrington seem to span from the time of the crime through the late 1980s, when reporters revisited the case, noting that it remained an unsolved mystery.

In one *Delaware County Daily Times* article from 1988, Ena Harrington sat down with a reporter in her Broomall home. She was described as a "short, attractive woman who looks younger than her forty years." The reporter, Nancy J. Holt, said the mother spoke softly about Gretchen. "It's never really over," Ena Harrington explained to Holt as she rocked in what was described as a "colonial-style chair." "You never really forget it."

In that same interview, Ena acknowledged that the only way the family would ever know what happened was if police found the murderer.

Reverend Harrington told the *County Leader* after his daughter's body was found in October 1975 that his devastated family would "pick up the pieces" and move forward with their lives. He said he, his wife and three other children would "carry on" with the help of their strong religious faith. "We're the kind of people who can do that," he told the newspaper.

In a 1988 interview with the *Delaware County Daily Times*, Reverend Harrington reiterated the family's desire to continue to soldier on. "The day my wife came home from Bryn Mawr Hospital [with the newborn baby, Jessyca], Gretchen was murdered," he told John Roman of the *Daily Times* in an August 15, 1988 story. "We've never forgotten but simply have had to go on with our lives." In that interview, Harrington seemed to appeal to the family members of his daughter's killer. "I've always been persuaded there's somebody who knows something that happened," he told Roman. "Probably the person involved is a relative and simply don't want to expose somebody who's precious to them."

Reverend Harrington went on to tell Roman that he and Ena were trying to raise their youngest daughter, Jessyca, without being too overprotective. They didn't want to make "life abnormal for Jessyca—a jail for her by overprotecting her," he said. "I think we succeeded," he said of Jessyca's ability to lead a normal life in the 1988 interview. "She's aware and she's not morbid about it or anything." He added, "We have several photos of Gretchen in the house. We treat Gretchen really just as though life had gone on. As a Christian, I don't regard Gretchen as dead.…She's one of my four daughters."

Reverend Harrington, in the 1988 interview, said Jessyca was in a program for advanced students and was "doing very well in school." "She's basically a musician; she sings in plays, in the choir and band at school," he said then. "Tragedy hasn't held her back."

Myers painted a different picture of what the tragedy did to her and her family. She said her family never really discussed what happened that August day, and she wonders about the damage that silence caused them. "My parents either forgot or weren't willing to discuss it," she said. She understands why but is not sure she agrees with the strategy. "You have to go on with your life," she said. "But it's incredibly difficult."

Keiser Watson said the Harringtons became reclusive in Broomall in the years following the crime. "They never came outside—we never saw them again," she said of Gretchen's sisters. "I think their parents were too afraid to let them out. I barely saw the mom again." Keiser Watson said she noticed that Reverend Harrington had undergone a dramatic change on the rare occasions she saw him after Gretchen's death. She said their neighbors had unfairly speculated over the following months and years that he had something to do with his daughter's tragic end. Reverend Harrington was never named as a suspect in the crime, according to Marple police. "His hair went from dark to silverish in that next year," Keiser Watson said. "He was a different person. He was a different man. He was old."

The change went beyond hair color within the family. Myers said the prevailing sadness that descended on her family made her angry. "I was angry about everything," she said. "I was angry my parents weren't my parents anymore. Kids at school didn't talk to me. Mostly, I was angry because my life wasn't like it used to be like." She said the kids at Delaware County Christian School had no idea what to say to her, so they didn't say anything. Myers did fondly remember two friends who helped her get through the school years there. As for the kids who ignored her, she finally understands why. "I've forgiven them," she said of her schoolmates. "I know they're really sorry."

Myers decided not to keep her sister's death a taboo subject in her own home. She said her son and daughters mourned the aunt they never knew. "My son was devastated by it," she said. "He asked to keep her picture in his room." The depths of Myers' devastation slowly came out over the years. She thought visiting the Marple police twenty years ago for more answers unleashed years of pent-up grief. "I really felt I went to the police because I needed more information," Myers said. "My parents weren't able to talk to me about it."

Myers was later diagnosed with post-traumatic stress disorder. Delving into the murder sent her into a downward emotional spiral that lasted ten years. She spent a year in bed. She said she used to look up the stages of grief and ask herself where she was. "I'm still angry," she said at the time the authors of this book spoke to her. Acceptance was a long time coming. "I've dealt with it," she said. "I'm not looking to solve a crime that's been cold case for forty-five years."

Myers credits her daughter Sarah Myers with helping her when she was bedridden with delayed grief and trauma. Sarah said she's proud of her mom for talking about her sister's death because it has helped with the healing process. She said, "My siblings and I knew growing up we had an aunt that was murdered, but it wasn't something that was discussed often or frequently." Sarah Myers continued, "My grandparents are very quiet about it. They don't bring it up. That's the space that they need." Sarah said she didn't remember her aunts Zoe and Jessyca discussing it either. But she called it "a moving force in their life." "It impacted everything," Sarah Myers said. Sarah Myers remembered playing in the neighborhood and coming home too late one day. Her mother panicked and feared something had happened to her daughter. "She was distraught and panicked and calling every person," Sarah Myers said.

Sarah Myers watched her mother become hospitalized for depression. The road to recovery has been a long one, but therapy and talking about the tragedy has helped her mother, Sarah Myers said. "She was hospitalized while I was in fourth grade," she said. "I was really mad about it when I was kid. I remember sitting next to her when she was in bed."

Though Myers painted a picture of parents who became distant after Gretchen's death, Sarah Myers doesn't share the same sentiment about Reverend and Ena Harrington. "I want people to know that my grandparents are amazing and incredibly resilient people," she said. "I'm honored to be their grandchild. They have so much love in their hearts." She added, "It didn't make them people who couldn't love their grandchildren. Some of my favorite memories are with them." She called them "very fun grandparents" and said that when she and brother were dropped off at the Harringtons' home for a week, "they would give us tools—give my brother and I a hammer and nails and saws and would say, 'Go build something.'"

Reverend Harrington's obituary gave a little insight into the relationship he had with his grandchildren. It mentions he was a talented amateur photographer, as evidenced by his Exacto cameras, still enjoyed by his granddaughters. "They [the Harringtons] only existed from a place of love—in my experience," Sarah Myers said.

Reverend and Ena Harrington lived with youngest daughter, Jessyca, in the suburban Philadelphia town of Abington until Reverend Harington's death in November 2021. His obituary named Gretchen as preceding him in death, but the writeup of his life focused on many positives, even shedding a little light on his many interests, including Johnny Cash, Chet Atkins, James Galway and classical Spanish guitar and his talent for gardening and woodworking.

Ena Harrington declined another request to talk about Gretchen after her husband's death. She, however, said she would read this book. "Mom needs to deal with that and not bring up old pain right now," Myers said of her father's passing.

Along with the Harrington family, the Reformed Presbyterian Church community is mourning the loss of Reverend Harrington. On hearing of Reverend Harrington's death, Matt Dyck, the pastor of Hillside Reformed Presbyterian Church in Almonte, Ontario, wrote that Reverend Harrington quickly became "an honorary Canadian…with that Canuck-beard and his 'pirate-like' boisterous laughter."

When Matt and other Canadian men feel the stress of ministry, they reminisce about Reverend Harrington's classes, wrote Reverend Edgar wrote in the obituary. "He was father to us all. He was notorious for cracking the odd joke during apologetics class, as he would expose the 'foolish' thinking of some world view," Dyck was quoted as saying. "But in and through it all was always the love of Christ and a big pastor's heart. He taught us to be more than good theologians."

4

MARPLE TOWNSHIP

From Sleepy Hamlet to Modern Suburb

An exodus of Philadelphians out of the city, growing transportation options and the post–World War II building boom transformed Marple Township from a sleepy country hamlet into a bedroom community for the City of Brotherly Love. Large retail establishments have long had a presence in the community following the migration from the rowhouse and postage stamp–sized lots in Philadelphia to the spacious split-levels on quarter-acre lots. Yet some of the small-town feeling still exists, although some common neighborhood names from the past, such as Larchmont and Marple Gardens, seem to have disappeared as longtime residents passed and newer, younger residents moved it.

There are a handful family-owned businesses that have existed there for decades and continue to prosper, including the Original Thunderbird Steakhouse, the Country Squire Diner, Drexel Hill Pizza, S. Pancoast Topsoil and Mulches, Italian Delite, the Hungry A and Irving A. Miller Real Estate. Many local and loved business closed years ago, including Bessie Parker's candy store, the small neighborhood Acme supermarket and the Broomall Pharmacy. Newer small businesses continue to operate in the single and strip storefronts and converted pre–World War II houses that line West Chester Pike between Church Lane and Malin Road.

"I'd like to think it is a small town, but it's clearly not,'" said Seth Pancoast, who lives in Marple and whose family has lived in the township since the 1700s. "The vibe is different. It just feels different....There are some great little businesses that people try to patronize, and I think everyone does a

Lawrence Road looking south toward West Chester Pike on August 15, 1975. *Marple Township Police Department.*

good job with that," Pancoast said. "But that stuff is kind of going away because the little places competing with the big places is tough."

To understand what Marple Township looked like when Gretchen Harrington went missing in August 1975, one has to take a brief look at how it evolved from a colonial settlement in the late seventeenth century to a small country crossroads community and then the suburban Philadelphia enclave it is today.

Long inhabited by a branch of the Lenni Lenape tribe, Marple Township was, in the seventeenth century, inhabited by Quakers who had been subjected to harassment from the Church of England for failing to pay tithes or attend services. One of these members of the Society of Friends was William Penn, who, in 1681, obtained land that later became the state of Pennsylvania as payment for a debt owed to his father by King Charles II. Penn, the namesake of Pennsylvania and founder of the City of Philadelphia, gave settlers the opportunity to buy or rent land for farming. Many who could not afford the price worked as servants to pay for their passage to the area.

One of these indentured servants was Thomas Massey, who was born in the village of Marpoole in Cheshire, England. Massey arrived in Chester at the age of twenty and became an indentured servant to Francis Stanfield, one of the three largest landholders in what became Marple Township. After fulfilling his indenture, Massey received a total of one hundred acres of land—fifty each from Stanfield and Penn. He married Phebe Taylor in 1692 and four years later purchased three hundred acres of land from James Stanfield, the son of Francis, and established his "plantation" there in Marple Township, building his house that fronts Lawrence Road. As the family expanded and changed, the house underwent a series of expansions and alterations.

Enveloped almost entirely by the Lawrence Park development, the house faced demolition when a descendant, Lawrence M.C. Smith, bought the house and one acre of land in 1964 and gave it to Marple Township for restoration. Today, the house sits on just one acre, but volunteers give tours and demonstrations of colonial living there and maintain the gardens from the period.

Before the Revolutionary War, many of the area's early farms gave way to homes where weavers, millers, joiners and tanners plied their crafts. Marple was not the scene of any notable battles or skirmishes, as it was against the Quaker faith to take an oath or participate in a conflict. But the community's farms were raided by the British and Continental armies, which stole food, clothing and livestock.

In 1834, a group of local residents belonging to the Middletown Presbyterian congregation decided to build a church of their own in Marple, making Marple Presbyterian Church the first and oldest church in the township.

Marple remained largely rural through the 1800s. Mills and tanneries operated there, and small villages where commerce was concentrated emerged. Broomall, the area centered on present-day West Chester Pike and Route 320, became the crossroads of Marple. A post office was built there and named for Judge John M. Broomall, a congressman from 1862 to 1870 and a friend and supporter of Abraham Lincoln.

In the early 1900s, a trolley line linking Philadelphia and West Chester was established. It connected what was then the nation's third-largest city with the outlying countryside west of the city limits. Residents could travel faster than ever before, and the line would eventually contribute to the suburbanization of the township. Trolley service ended in 1954, and the tracks were removed so that West Chester Pike could be widened from two to four lanes to accommodate the growing amount of vehicular traffic.

The intersection of West Chester Pike and Sproul Road as it appeared around the turn of the twentieth century.

Marple and next-door Newtown Township experienced some new construction in the 1920s, but it was not until the 1950s that full-scale postwar suburbanization arrived in Marple Township. This was most notable in two developments, Lawrence Park and Rose Tree Woods, where veterans who were arriving home from World War II could use the GI Bill to secure low-interest mortgages with a small down payment. "The GIs had an advantage because they were going back into a job and were able to get a mortgage fairly easily," said Peter L. Goss, professor emeritus of architectural history in the College of Architecture and Planning at the University of Utah. "It was inevitable due to the end of the war. All of the returning GIs needed housing, and they were either married or were going to get married and start families."

Marple grew rapidly, from four thousand residents in 1950 to twenty thousand in 1960. It had nearly twenty-four thousand residents as of 2018, according to census data.

The need for public safety services grew with the township. At first, the Pennsylvania State Police would send patrols through the area randomly.

At one time, there was a resident state trooper who was responsible for handling crime in the Marple, Newtown and Edgemont Townships. At the start of World War II, as the population approached three thousand, the township began paying elected constables to patrol the township on a full- and part-time basis. Lester Downs and Harry Eastburn patrolled the township in their own vehicles and were compensated based on the amount of time they spent on patrols. Various U.S. Army units that were stationed in the area assisted the constables.

The Marple Township Police Department was established in 1948, with Downs appointed as the first chief. Several men were hired to provide twenty-four-hour-long patrols. The first police station was located on the second floor of the Broomall Fire Company Firehouse on West Chester Pike and has moved three times since: to the then-new municipal building in the 1950s, to the old Marple Public Library building next to the municipal building and then to a modern facility in the Lawrence Park Industrial Center as the department ranks rose from thirty officers in the late 1960s to just under thirty-nine as of this writing.

The Broomall Fire Company was formed on December 18, 1922, at the urging of Ernest Dupille. The initial group of twenty-six men met again on January 8, 1923, to approve a constitution and company by-laws. During this meeting, Mr. Dupille was elected president, and W.E. Clark Sr. was elected the first fire chief. A lot was purchased on West Chester Pike near Sproul Road for a firehouse, which the tradesman in the company built themselves in 1924. In August 1923, the official charter of the Broomall Fire Company was adopted and signed by sixty men. A manually operated gong was received from the Oakmont Fire Company in Havertown to act as an alarm, and it was placed on the recently purchased lot. Two hand extinguishers were received from the Highland Park Fire Company in Upper Darby, and resident Alphonso Fox donated a hand-drawn hose reel.

Over the years, the all-volunteer fire company purchased equipment to meet the needs of the growing community and moved to larger quarters twice in the following years. The second firehouse was built at West Chester Pike and North Malin Road and dedicated on November 2, 1957. The fire company dedicated its current home, built on the site of the former Marple Grade School, on November 2, 2019.

The Marple Township Ambulance Corps was founded in March 1949 by a group of concerned citizens who realized the need for efficient emergency care in the community. The first vehicle owned by the corps was a used Pontiac ambulance that was donated by the Broomall Businessmen's

The sales brochure for Lawrence Park. Developer Ralph Bodek touted the "suburban charm" of the development, with its wide, winding streets, park and play areas and shopping center, to draw buyers to his community. *Joe Bodek.*

Association. The ambulance was originally kept in a building owned by George Parker Sr., one of the founding members of the corps. This building was located in the area of what is now John's Auto Body on West Chester Pike. The corps was headquartered there until the building at Sproul and Harding Roads was constructed in 1960. In order to keep pace with the growing need for emergency services, a second ambulance was added in the mid-1950s. The corps is now located in the former Broomall Fire Company Firehouse at West Chester Pike and Malin Road.

The two largest developments in Marple Township are Lawrence Park and Rose Tree Woods. Both developments were marketed to young couples with growing families who were lured to the areas with spacious homes on large lots, low monthly mortgage payments, safe neighborhoods and good schools.

LAWRENCE PARK

The land that became Lawrence Park was purchased by Ralph Bodek, a Philadelphia-based builder who also built Colonial Park, a five-hundred-home subdivision in Springfield, Delaware County; Aldan Park, a community of one hundred duplexes in Aldan; Westbrook Park, a development of two hundred rowhouses in Clifton Heights; and apartment buildings in Upper Darby.

Bodek was the son of Jenny and Joseph Bodek, a builder and manager of apartment houses. He attended the University of Pennsylvania, receiving a

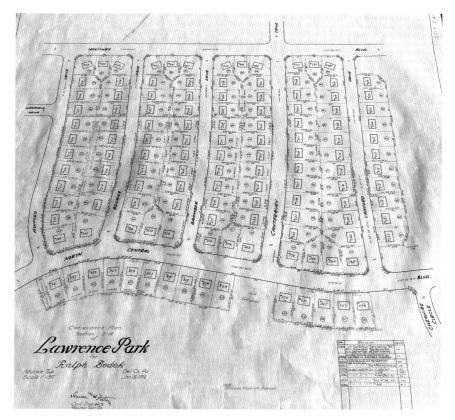

An engineering drawing that shows some of the streets in the Lawrence Park development. The engineering work for the development was done by H. Gilroy Damon Associates of Sharon Hill, Pennsylvania. The firm has provided engineering services for several Delaware County communities since its founding in 1894. *Mike Mathis.*

bachelor's degree in economics in 1937. Bodek worked for his father, helping manage the family's real estate holdings, then joined the U.S. Naval Air Force during World War II.

After the war, Bodek worked a series of jobs, including spending two years as a police reporter for the *Philadelphia Inquirer*. He also sold insurance and briefly owned an advertising agency before returning to work for his father.

For his largest residential project, Bodek purchased a six-hundred-acre tract of land for $900,000 that had been assembled in the 1930s by Samuel Robinson, the cofounder of Acme Markets. Bodek named it Lawrence Park, after the road that ran through the property.

Bodek eventually built 1,200 homes—mostly split-levels but also some colonials—on 420 acres between 1954 and 1963. Zoning requirements mandated that one-quarter of the 600 acres be set aside for industrial and commercial development and that another parcel be set aside for a school and parks. An advertisement in the *Philadelphia Inquirer* boasted that Lawrence Park was "600 acres of suburban charm with wide, winding streets carefully designed to eliminate dangerous intersections and provide a maximum of safety for you and your loved ones."

Some accounts say that Bodek first saw some form of a split-level house in California and that he invented the then-modern split-level houses that now dominate Lawrence Park. However, many of Bodek's contemporaries were building them through the Philadelphia area, perhaps most notable were Robert Scarborough, who constructed split-level houses in his Kenwood and Barclay Farm developments in Delaware Township, New Jersey (now Cherry Hill), and Harry Goodwin, who built Kingston Estates, also in Delaware Township. Other developers constructed split-level homes on a smaller scale in the Philadelphia area.

Ground was broken for the Lawrence Park Shopping Center on June 6, 1956. Built on thirty-five acres at Sproul and Lawrence Roads, the center had parking for three thousand vehicles and included a Food Fair grocery store, a bowling alley, a branch of the N. Snellenburg and Co. department store chain, W.T Grant Co., F.W. Woolworth Co., a movie theater and several

Houses under construction on Dorset Drive in Lawrence Park in September 1955. The street is located not far from where Gretchen Harrington disappeared. *MediaHistoricArchives.org.*

Left: Westbourne Drive's intersection at Robinson Drive in Lawrence Park in the late 1950s. *Mike Mathis.*

Right: A house on Cornwall Drive in Lawrence Park in June 1969. *Mike Mathis.*

smaller stores, including a florist, barbershop, beauty salon and hardware store. The shopping complex was formally dedicated in October 1957.

The Lawrence Park Theater opened on October 10, 1957, with Fred Astaire in *Silk Stockings*. It had one thousand seats and a forty-two-foot-wide screen. It was designed by architectural firm Thalheimer and Weitz and was operated by the Abel and Silber circuit. It was twinned on November 22, 1978, and was acquired by the Sameric Corp. It closed in October 1991, and as of this writing, the building houses a bookstore.

The 150-acre Lawrence Park Industrial Center opened in 1961, next to the Lawrence Park Shopping Center. To market Lawrence Park, Bodek authored *How and Why People Buy Houses* (1958), which compared split-level houses to rowhouses, duplexes, ranch houses and two-story colonials. Those interviewed for the book were families who bought homes in Lawrence Park. They were asked what considerations went into their housing decisions and what factors influenced them, such as advertising and friends' suggestions.

Among the advertising vehicles Bodek used to reach potential buyers was *Life* magazine, one of the most powerful sales tools of that era. Bodek purchased a large advertisement in that publication and also bought display advertisment space in local newspapers.

"The split-level is not regarded as extreme or unconventional as is the ranch house, but it is thought to be comfortable and modern," Bodek wrote in *How and Why People Buy Houses*. "The split-level family thinks of itself as progressive, even to the point, in some cases, of 'casual living.'" He concluded:

The playback confirmed the fact that people consider the split-level style as a compromise between the ranch and the conventional two-story house. The two-story home is too conservative in concept, represents too big a social jump, and is too inefficient as a functional living unit. The ranch is too radical, although admittedly efficient as a living machine. The split-level home is modern, functional and efficient, but not too far in "left field" as regards styling.

Bodek also observed that those who bought houses in Lawrence Park experienced an elevation in their social status that didn't exist when they lived in a rowhouse or apartment. "You are getting somewhere when you own your own home," one respondent said. "You are successful, you want something to show for it."

While small suburban subdivisions existed outside of American cities in the early twentieth century, it wasn't until after World War II that the idea of large-scale development of single-family homes took off. Goss said modern suburban development exploded after World War II outside the population centers on the East and West Coasts, including New York and Los Angeles.

The most notable and famous of these modern suburbs was Levittown, which was built starting in the late 1940s on potato farms in central Long Island, New York. Levitt and Sons Inc. was founded by Abraham Levitt in 1929; his sons William and Alfred served as the company's president and chief architect and planner. The firm built more than sixteen thousand houses in New York and built two other Levittowns, one in Pennsylvania and the other in New Jersey, with more than seventeen thousand and twelve thousand home, respectively. "They were developing something that hadn't been developed before," Goss said of the Levitts. "Levitt set the whole thing up for [future] suburban development to happen."

This plaque was installed in front of the Lawrence Park Theater when the Lawrence Park Shopping Center was dedicated on October 9, 1957. The plaque is now located outside a bookstore where the theater was once located. *Mike Mathis.*

Bodek's obituary in the October 16, 1998 *Philadelphia Inquirer* noted that he once said that he was fascinated by Levitt's concept of the assembly line process of building houses, in which, unlike a traditional production line through which a product passes a worker,

Top: The Lawrence Park Shopping Center as it appeared in 1965. *Joe Bodek.*

Bottom: The Lawrence Park Theater, pictured just before its grand opening on October 10, 1957. *Mike Mathis.*

the framers, plumbers and electricians moved from house to house. In a December 10, 1991 *Philadelphia Inquirer* story, Bodek said that while he liked the production line concept, he did not like the actual houses. "I thought his units were a little bit on the skimpy side," Bodek told the newspaper.

Copying another facet of Levitt's three developments, Bodek named the streets in Lawrence Park in alphabetical order.

Bodek spent his later years developing commercial properties and shopping centers in Florida. He died on October 10, 1998, at the age of eighty-four.

Rose Tree Woods

Frank Facciolo and William Barrett began developing Rose Tree Woods in 1948 on the former estate of A. Atwater Kent, an inventor and radio manufacturer. The A. Atwater Kent Manufacturing Company was the largest producer of radios in the nation in the early twentieth century, employing twelve thousand people and manufacturing nearly one million radio sets annually. The company closed in 1936. When he died in 1949, A. Atwater Kent held ninety-three patents for improvements in automobile ignition systems and electronics.

The Rose Tree Woods development included more than 1,100 homes, but it has been most distinguished by its one-story California ranch–style homes, which are lovingly called "the flattops" by their owners and Marple natives. The company previously built homes in Paoli, King of Prussia, Coatesville and in other areas of Bucks, Chester, Delaware and Montgomery Counties.

The developers, who met while they were students at Villanova University, donated ten acres for the Rose Tree Woods Swim Club. Facciolo also attended law school at Villanova and was a real estate broker.

To sell his houses, Facciolo built models in strategic locations around Philadelphia. "I remember when they were selling them so fast that they just built a wooden platform and put a candy-striped canopy over it, and people would drive up and sign the papers right there," Bill Spiller Sr., who for many years operated a family tire business on Sproul Road across from Facciolo's development, told the *Inquirer* in a 1997 interview.

Facciolo died on March 25, 2002, at the age of seventy-eight; as of this writing, his real estate office, located in a single split-level house that he built in 1948 on Sproul Road near Paxon Hollow Road, is still open.

WHILE A HANDFUL OF long-standing business still exist, Marple Township's first suburbanites would hardly recognize the community today. The farmstands and fields that once stood on several street corners, including a prominent corner across the street from Frank Facciolo's office, are now gone.

The Mid-County Expressway, Interstate 476, which is known locally as the Blue Route, connects the Pennsylvania Turnpike and Interstate 95. Its construction was first discussed in the late 1920s, shelved during the Great Depression and then stalled through the 1950s, 1960s and 1970s because of community opposition. The highway opened in December 1991, bringing additional traffic and development. A major interchange is located at West Chester Pike, where a shopping center, convenience store with a gas station and a hotel are now located. The hotel is perched on a hillside overlooking the old Pathmark supermarket, now the site of an outpatient health facility. The shopping center, convenience store and hotel are within walking distance of the church where Reverend Harrington preached and the house where Gretchen lived with her parents and sisters.

Both the church and the house appear unchanged—except for the addition of a metal roof and some siding on the house. Though they front busy Lawrence Road, the backyard abuts Darby Creek, a tributary of the Delaware River. Perhaps not so different than it did in 1975, the backyard offers kids a place to play and explore. A trampoline, kids' bikes and balls were all visible on a recent walk by the property.

5

VIOLENT TIMES

T ed Bundy. John Wayne Gacy. The Zodiac Killer. Son of Sam. The Hillside Strangler. They are America's most notorious murderers of the late 1960s and 1970s—an era now considered the heyday of the *serial killer*, a term coined by the FBI for predators who left a trail of bodies—in some cases, the bodies were never found.

Many of their victims' names are long forgotten, if people ever knew them. But the killers themselves have cemented a place in the psyche of millions. They've spawned books, movies, obsessive "fans" and even copycat killers. It's tough to turn the channel on cable television or peruse the internet without finding some mention of one or more of these notorious monsters. Legions of true crime fans keep their names alive.

Criminal justice expert Peter Vronsky, in his book *Sons of Cain: A History of Serial Killers from the Stone Age to the Present*, makes the case that there have always been serial killers. "But we just do not have a record of them because there was no formal law enforcement agencies in the form of 'police' as we know it, nor a printing press that distributed news or accounts of serial murder in the way there was by Jack the Ripper's time in 1888," he told *Rolling Stone* in a 2021 story. The story asked: "Why Were There So Many Serial Killers Between 1970 and 2000—and Where Did They Go?" Vronsky wrote that during the great witch hunt in Western Europe between the fifteenth and eighteenth centuries, serial killers were put on trial as werewolves.

Despite serial killers having likely been around forever, the mania surrounding these mass murderers was hardly a phenomenon in 1975, when Gretchen was kidnapped and murdered. Until then, perhaps only Charles Manson and the Boston Strangler captured the fascination of the American public.

"The '70s and '80s were absolutely the era of the serial killer," said David Schmid, an English professor at the University of Buffalo whose areas of expertise include pop culture, celebrity and crime. "Today, we're in a very different kind of situation….We still have that sense of anxiety. But the serial killer has tended to take a backseat to the school shooter, the random shooter at the supermarket." Schmid said it wasn't until the late 1970s that people became more aware of abductions and murders by strangers. It was then that he said the FBI "claimed ownership" of serial murder, alerting the public that children faced dangers from predators lurking about.

In the 1970s, it wasn't unusual for people to leave their doors unlocked in many communities. Hitchhiking was a common—and almost romanticized—practice. Children walked to school alone. No one told them they weren't safe. Schmid said that's why cases like Gretchen's resonated so much in communities like Broomall. "It seems to sort of mark a sea change—from a period where you can take your safety for granted to now a new situation where you can't do that anymore," said Schmid, the author of *Murder Culture* and *From the Locked Room to the Globe: Space in Crime Fiction*.

But Schmid said the awareness—and fear—of serial killers was disproportionate to the actual danger. Crimes by the likes of Bundy, who went on a spree of terror across the United States, were still extremely unusual. In Marple Township, any crime, let alone a serial murder, was a rare occurrence. Though it is located only about thirteen miles from the Philadelphia city line, the quiet suburb's recorded crimes didn't go far beyond nuisance and property crimes. Even today, it remains a relatively safe suburb, despite its growth and a rise in crime in Philadelphia during the pandemic.

But in the 1970s, safety may have been taken for granted. No one really expected a crime like kidnapping and murder to take place in Broomall. Children had the freedom to roam. So many people who lived in Marple or in other suburbs where murders occurred across the United States, had left the city in pursuit of a secure place to raise their children. The refrain "things like that don't happen here" was a mindset and a mantra.

But the random murder of a child definitely happened in Broomall, in nearby Media and in cities, towns and suburbs of all sizes across the county. There wasn't a twenty-four-hour news channel or nationwide media exhaustively covering such stories. They remained local—CNN didn't exist. Not to mention that police jurisdictions didn't have the means of sharing information about crimes through databases and email. Schmid calls such a lack of communication between police jurisdictions "linkage blindness." In some cases, criminals were well aware of the lack of information sharing and committed murders in different jurisdictions to take advantage of this weakness.

The names of convicted sex offenders topped the list of suspects in Gretchen's case as Marple police scoured the community for leads on who abducted and killed the girl. In a time before sex offender registries, police had to comb through court records to come up with lists of convicted sex offenders nearby. The Harrington file at the Marple Township Police Department held several lists of such men and their offenses. The file also contained newspaper clippings about murders of young girls throughout the country.

Even Henry Lee Lucas, a notorious self-proclaimed serial killer who confessed to killing as many as six hundred people, was briefly among the suspects, said Chief Brandon Graeff. Lucas lived in nearby Chester County, Pennsylvania, at the time of Gretchen's disappearance and death. Lucas was convicted of eleven total murders. He was sentenced to death in Texas in 1984 for the 1979 murder of an unidentified woman who was known at the time as "Orange Socks" and was identified in 2019 as Debra Jackson. Lucas later recanted his confession, and citing a lack of evidence tying Lucas to the killing, then-governor George W. Bush commuted his death sentence in 1998. Lucas died of a heart attack in prison in 2001.

Some have even speculated that Ted Bundy may have been involved in Gretchen's and Wendy Eaton's deaths. Bundy was a student at Temple University in Philadelphia in the late 1960s. Bundy confessed to kidnapping, raping and killing more than thirty women in seven states between 1974 and 1978. Those who have tracked Bundy's crime rampage place him out west during the time of the Delaware County girls' murders. But it is now widely believed that Bundy may have been the culprit in the unsolved murders of two college students, Susan Davis and Elizabeth Perry, in 1969. The girls were murdered after going to the beach resort of Ocean City, New Jersey, for Memorial Day weekend. Ted Bundy attended Temple University for a semester at that time. He lived in Roxborough, Pennsylvania, with his grandparents. The couple also owned a home in Ocean City, according to a June 11, 2021 story in *MONTCO Today*, a suburban Philadelphia newspaper.

Bundy's killing spree and other high-profile cases made the abduction and murder of children and young women seem rampant in the 1970s. Among these highly publicized crimes was the infamous disappearance of the Lyon sisters in Wheaton, Maryland. On March 25, 1975, Katherine Mary Lyon, ten, and Sheila Lyon, twelve, walked to Wheaton Plaza, a shopping mall in suburban Washington, D.C. Walking to the mall, hanging out at the food court and strolling in and out of shops was a normal thing for teens to do at that time. Parents often dropped their kids off at the mall, a bowling alley or a movie theater. If you lived close enough to walk, that was even better.

The sisters, daughters of John Lyon, a well-known Washington radio personality, disappeared on that outing to the mall. They were never seen again, launching what became one of the most intense investigations in Maryland's history. The case, much like Gretchen's, changed the way both children and parents thought of their community. The busy suburbs of Washington, D.C., suddenly seemed dangerous. Kids who grew up with the mystery of the Lyons sisters' disappearance knew that it could easily have been them. "I remember it made Wheaton Mall seem scary," said Elena Paoli, a Wheaton native who was eleven at the time of the disappearance. "It made the prospect of going out alone with your friends scary—and our parents were very concerned."

A team of cold case investigators in Montgomery County, Maryland, made a break in the Lyons' case in 2013, leading them back to a 1975-era sketch of a man who was seen at the mall the day the girls disappeared. They focused on Lloyd Lee Welch Jr., who was in 2013 serving a long prison sentence in Delaware for child sexual abuse. He had been interviewed by police soon after the girls' abduction and was given a polygraph test. Then after the sketch triggered another look at Welch, Montgomery County police traveled to Delaware to interview him in prison thirteen times over two years.

Welch eventually pleaded guilty to two counts of first-degree murder for the abduction and murder of the Lyons girls in 2017. The other men suspected in the case died before the trial. The girls' bodies have never been found. "I hold out no reasonable hope the bodies of these young girls will ever be found," said Montgomery County state's attorney John McCarthy, who prosecuted Welch. McCarthy and Assistant State's Attorney Peter Feeney, who were interviewed for this book, said the remains are likely on Taylor's Mountain outside of Bedford, Virginia, where Welch family members still own property. They believe the girls bodies were burned in a bonfire that witnesses, including some of Welch's relatives, said went on for days. "It's interesting to note that [after an] exhaustive search by the FBI, state police, there was nothing," Feeney said. "Allegedly a tooth was found and lost."

McCarthy said police in 1975 didn't follow through with their suspicions of Welch. Instead, they focused more on reports of a man who was approaching kids at Wheaton Plaza with a tape recorder rather than the young man who was seen following them. That young man turned out to be Welch. The more than forty-year-old sketch of him remained in the evidence files but was ignored for decades. "That sketch is a dead ringer of Lloyd Lee Welch—a dead ringer," McCarthy said.

McCarthy said it's not unusual for police and the public to fixate on one detail and miss what may be a glaring piece of evidence. For example, he said reports of a white box truck trumped sightings of a Chevrolet Caprice when two snipers terrorized the Baltimore–Washington, D.C. area in 2002. People became focused on the white box truck, while the snipers, Lee Boyd Malvo and John Lee Muhammad, were actually using a Caprice for their crime spree.

McCarthy was teaching at a nearby high school when the Lyons sisters were snatched from Wheaton Plaza. Though he wasn't yet a prosecutor, he saw the impact on the community. "I think it changed everything. It changed the way people raised their children," McCarthy said. "The way children were reared in this community changed overnight."

Feeney said he used to walk for miles to go the mall. "It was a different era, but it changed overnight," Feeney said. "It became the locality of neurotic parents."

One thing McCarthy and Feeney discovered in their investigation of the Lyons case is just how many sexual predators were in the vicinity of Wheaton Plaza that day. Over the years, investigators came up with multiple suspects in the case and unearthed the "seedy underbelly" of Montgomery County, Maryland. "It really is an extremely bizarre circumstance," McCarthy said. "There were multiple child predators in the Wheaton area."

He said the investigation never touched on other kidnappings or murders in the mid-Atlantic around the time of the Lyons sisters' disappearance, including Gretchen's five months after the Maryland crime. Though there wasn't a sex offender registry at the time, police collected information on similar crimes and on suspects with records that included sexual abuse of children.

The Gretchen Harrington case file is filled with news of such cases— some solved and others still stone cold. A yellowed newspaper clipping in the file tells of the murder of a ten-year-old girl just a month after Gretchen's disappearance. Donna Ann Willoughby disappeared on

September 6, 1975, near her south Philadelphia home. Her mother reported her missing after she failed to return home from a neighborhood playground, according to a story in the *Philadelphia Inquirer*. The girl was found by three teenage boys a week later in a thicket near the city's Gulf Refinery; she had been stabbed to death.

Marple police detectives met on October 2, 1975, with their counterparts in Philadelphia to "compare notes" on the Harrington and Willoughby crimes. That case has apparently never been solved either. In the Willoughby case, once again, the same refrain could be heard after the girl's murder—the belief that a good ZIP code could prevent anything bad from happening. "I never expected anything like this to happen in our neighborhood," Sharon Williams, then thirteen, told the *Philadelphia Inquirer*. "I saw her [Donna Ann Willoughby] the day she disappeared. She was riding her brother's red bike and she was buying an ice cream cone from the truck." There were reports that the girl was seen in a blue and white car with a man and woman and several other children.

Among the cases that baffled investigators from a year before Gretchen's disappearance was that of fourteen-year-old Margaret Fox, who left her home in Burlington City, New Jersey, on the morning of June 24, 1974, boarded a bus to go to a babysitting job in Mount Holly, New Jersey, and vanished. At the time of her disappearance, Margaret had just graduated from the eighth grade at St. Paul School in Burlington City.

Several days earlier, when Margaret responded to a newspaper advertisement, she spoke to a man who called himself John Marshall and offered her forty dollars a week, plus bus fare, to watch his five-year-old son for about four hours, according to an account in the *Burlington County Times*. Joe Fox, Margaret's eleven-year-old brother, walked his sister to the bus stop and watched her board the bus. Marshall said he would pick her up in his red Volkswagen at the bus stop at High and Mill Streets in Mount Holly and that he or his wife would bring her home by 2:00 p.m. or 2:30 p.m.

Margaret's father, David Fox, spoke to the man and asked that Margaret be allowed to call them from Marshall's house to let them know she had arrived, the newspaper reported. When their daughter did not call, David and Mary Fox, Margaret's mother, dialed what was supposedly John Marshall's home phone number. Instead, they reached a pay phone outside a grocery store on Route 38 in Lumberton, New Jersey, a township next to Mount Holly, the newspaper reported.

Investigators established early on that it did not appear that Margaret ran away. The next day, police retraced the girl's steps and showed her picture to about two hundred people. Several people remembered seeing her, but their recollections did not produce viable leads, according to news accounts. In the following years, the police investigated numerous tips as well as many men in the area who were named John Marshall or owned red cars. In all, the police developed, investigated and cleared twelve persons of interest.

The FBI, in 2019, announced a $25,000 reward for information that led to the arrest or conviction of whoever was responsible for Margaret's disappearance. When the FBI announced the reward, it also released an audio recording of a person who called Fox's parents and demanded $10,000 shortly after she disappeared. On the recording, a man can be heard saying, "$10,000 might be a lot of bread, but your daughter's life is the buttered topping." The Fox family also received a note with the same text.

Gretchen Harrington's disappearance was one of several disappearances of young girls that Delaware County authorities were investigating in the spring and summer of 1975. Investigators were never able to connect them.

One of the most publicized cases was that of Wendy Eaton, who disappeared near her house on Moccasin Trail in Middletown Township on May 17, 1975, a week before her sixteenth birthday. It was reported that she was headed to Media, Delaware County's seat, to buy a gift for her older brother. She was last seen by neighbors near Indian Lane and Media Station Road. Eaton was never found, and she was officially declared dead in August 1983.

But the cold case suddenly seemed to be revived on May 17, 2021, the forty-sixth anniversary of Eaton's disappearance. State police searched and excavated a wooded area behind a home at Indian Lane and Media Station Road after receiving new leads in the case. It has now been ruled a homicide.

After being reached by phone and email, Wendy Eaton's sister Nancy declined to talk about the case in February 2022. She said it was still a great source of pain some forty-six years later.

Wendy Eaton's father, Roland L. Eaton Jr., a Sun Oil Co. marketing executive, was very outspoken in his quest to find his daughter and compelled police to do more to find out what happened to her. Eaton died in 2007 at the age of eighty-four.

Eaton told the *Delaware County Daily Times* in August 1975 that he had called the FBI for help in finding his daughter Wendy, Gretchen Harrington and two other girls who had gone missing around the same time, Denise Seaman, seventeen, and Mary Ann Lees, fifteen. The newspaper reported that Eaton had written then–FBI director Clarence Kelley and urged his fellow Delaware County residents to write to Pennsylvania senators Hugh

Scott and Richard S. Schweiker, "asking them to intervene in our behalf." Eaton said in the interview, "What's my problem and the Harringtons' today can well be somebody else's tomorrow."

Eaton compared and contrasted the lack of federal intervention in the Delaware County cases to the FBI's extensive efforts in finding missing labor union boss Jimmy Hoffa. Hoffa, the president of the International Brotherhood of Teamsters from 1957 to 1975, disappeared in 1975 and was never found. It's widely believed that Hoffa, who had connections to the Mafia, was murdered by the organized crime syndicate. Rumors about where Hoffa's body might be abound and include a persistent tale that he was buried in the endzone of the old Giants Stadium in the Meadowlands Sports Complex in New Jersey. The stadium opened in 1976, one year after Hoffa vanished. Though several movies and numerous books profess to tell the truth about what happened to Hoffa, it remains one of the perplexing mysteries of American history.

Eaton said the FBI was investigating the Hoffa case despite the fact that there was no evidence of an abduction or ransom demand connected. "What the hell do we have, two sets of laws in this country—one for the bad guys and one for the good guys?" Eaton asked then. "This is no longer just my situation. To me, it's a community situation. How many girls have we got out there who are missing?" Eaton was referring to Gretchen and two other Delaware County girls who went missing around the time, Denise Seaman, seventeen, and Debra Jean Delozier, twenty. He also mentioned the murders of two Upper Darby girls whose bodies were found in the Schuylkill River in 1975 and the abduction of another Colwyn girl whose body was found in Marcus Hook, Pennsylvania. "What do we have to do to get assistance from these people?" Eaton asked in the *Daily Times* story. "It's possible that if the FBI had gotten involved [in these other disappearances] this latest tragedy [Gretchen's disappearance], could have been averted."

Police then and now consider potential links exist between the Eaton and Harrington case. That was never made public but was disclosed to the Harrington family during the investigation. The other cases, which are known as the Tinicum Marsh murders, have never been solved. The bodies of Mary Ann Lees, Denise Seaman, Layne Dorothy Spicer and Debra Jean Delozier were all eventually found in the Tinicum Swamp and Philadelphia's Schuylkill River, but their killers were never caught or brought to justice.

The body of Seaman, a seventeen-year-old from Colwyn, was found in a shallow grave by hunters in Tinicum Marsh near Philadelphia International Airport on October 17, 1975. Published accounts state that she had been shot in the head with a .22-caliber pistol, and her jaw was broken. Seaman was last seen alive on May 10, 1975.

Seaman was at one time a neighbor of Mary Ann Lees, fifteen, and Layne Dorothy Spicer, fifteen, who were both from the Stonehurst section of Upper Darby. They were reported missing on March 27, 1975, and were found shot to death in the Schuykill River in Southwest Philadelphia on March 31, 1975.

Delozier, a twenty-year-old from Collingdale, was reported missing on August 16, 1975, one day after Gretchen Harrington disappeared. A story in the *Delaware County Daily Times* mentioned that both disappeared within a block of their homes in the same week. But the story quoted officers who said there were likely no links between the cases. Delozier's remains were discovered by hunters in Tinicum Marsh on January 17, 1976, not far from where Seaman's remains were found. Like in Seaman's case, a .22-caliber bullet was lodged in Delozier's skull, and her jaw was broken, according to published reports.

Another girl, Susan Jamison, a fifteen-year-old from Colwyn, was found beaten and unconscious with a rope around her neck in a truck parking lot in Trainer on November 12, 1975, two days after she was reported missing.

Police believed the killings were linked to the Warlock motorcycle gang, a notorious Philadelphia biker group that, to this day, is linked to drugs and murder. Their killers were never caught or prosecuted.

The Tinicum Marsh murders have long made the swampy land near the Philadelphia International Airport a mysterious place. But today, it is known as the John Heinz National Wildlife Refuge at Tinicum and is part of the U.S. Fish and Wildlife Service's National Wildlife Refuge System. The one-thousand-acre refuge boasts ten miles of trails and is considered the largest freshwater tidal marsh in Pennsylvania. It was named after the late Senator John Heinz in 1991 for his efforts to preserve the land. Heinz died in a plane crash in Lower Merion Township, just outside of Philadelphia, in 1991.

One of the earliest and most notorious cases in Marple Township was the murder of Benjamin Panfilo D'Amore, fifty-three, who was gunned down in the driveway of his house on November 20, 1949. The house adjoined the State Road Nurseries, which D'Amore operated with his son-in-law on State Road near Sproul Road. The house and nursery were located in the area of the present Marple Crossroads Shopping Center.

Authorities charged that D'Amore's sons, John D'Amore, twenty-two, and Nicholas D'Amore, twenty-five, both of Philadelphia, had killed their father because, for years, he abused their mother, Concetta D'Amore, according to an account in the *Chester Times*. "I waited for years to do this—since I was six," Nicholas D'Amore told investigators. "He was always abusing mother. I knew this was the end....I didn't want him to get away." The younger brother said he had had a similar idea "since I was eight years old," the newspaper reported.

The case focused on the brothers' mental state, according to newspaper accounts. "There is no dispute that these boys killed their father," Judge William R. Toal, who presided over the five-day trial, told the panel of jurors before they adjourned to deliberate. "The real question for your determination is what was their mental state at the time of the killing?"

The brothers were acquitted by an all-female jury on January 10, 1950. Before discharging the jury, Judge Toal told them, "I still insist it was an unlawful killing because the law never justifies a killing."

Judge Toal's son, William R. Toal Jr., sat as a judge in Delaware County for many years. He retired in 2010 and died in September 2016 at the age of eighty-three.

The other two notable homicides that occurred in Marple Township remain unsolved.

The bullet-riddled body of Frank Forlini, the forty-three-year-old co-owner of a Darby Township concrete firm who lived in Upper Providence, was found slumped over the front seat of his pick-up truck in the parking lot of the K-Mart store on Reed Road on February 9, 1985. He had been shot in the head, once in the neck and three times in the chest, according to media accounts. The killing was possibly linked to organized crime.

More than three years before Gretchen Harrington's kidnapping and murder, Mary Hannig, thirty-nine, was shot and killed as she investigated a burglary at a neighbor's house near her North Sproul Road house on January 17, 1972. Police said Mrs. Hannig, a mother of four, told one of her daughters to call police and asked another teen daughter to go with her. But about halfway to the house, she told her daughter to return home and call the police, according to an account in the *Delaware County Daily Times*. She then confronted two men as they were stealing a color television from the house, according to the story. The Hannig girls heard their mother's voice and then a gunshot, the *Daily Times* reported. Police said Mrs. Hannig was able to provide some details about her assailants, including information about a getaway car, before she died from a bullet wound to the right side of her chest about a half-hour later at Haverford Hospital.

The location where the bullet-riddled body of Frank Forlini, the forty-three-year-old co-owner of a Darby Township concrete firm who lived in Upper Providence, was found slumped over the front seat of his pick-up truck in the parking lot of what was then a K-Mart discount store on Reed Road on February 9, 1985. He had been shot in the head, once in the neck and three times in the chest, according to media accounts. The killing was possibly linked to organized crime. In addition to the Harrington case, the Forlini case remains unsolved. *Mike Mathis.*

More than three years before Gretchen Harrington's kidnapping and murder, Mary Hannig, thirty-nine, was shot and killed as she investigated a burglary at a neighbor's house near her North Sproul Road house on January 17, 1972. In addition to the Harrington case, the Hannig case remains unsolved. *Mike Mathis.*

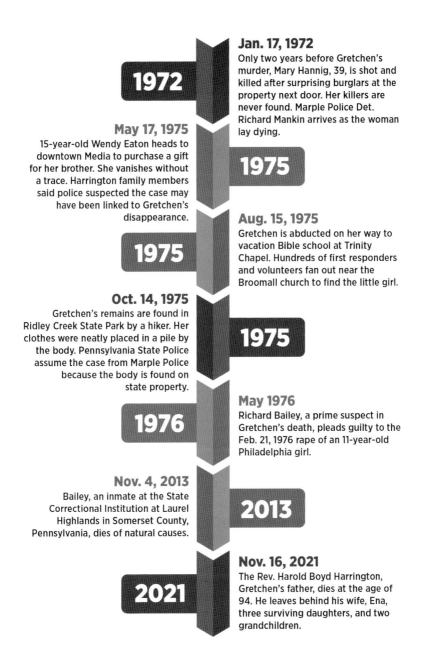

1972

Jan. 17, 1972
Only two years before Gretchen's murder, Mary Hannig, 39, is shot and killed after surprising burglars at the property next door. Her killers are never found. Marple Police Det. Richard Mankin arrives as the woman lay dying.

May 17, 1975
15-year-old Wendy Eaton heads to downtown Media to purchase a gift for her brother. She vanishes without a trace. Harrington family members said police suspected the case may have been linked to Gretchen's disappearance.

1975

Aug. 15, 1975
Gretchen is abducted on her way to vacation Bible school at Trinity Chapel. Hundreds of first responders and volunteers fan out near the Broomall church to find the little girl.

1975

Oct. 14, 1975
Gretchen's remains are found in Ridley Creek State Park by a hiker. Her clothes were neatly placed in a pile by the body. Pennsylvania State Police assume the case from Marple Police because the body is found on state property.

1975

May 1976
Richard Bailey, a prime suspect in Gretchen's death, pleads guilty to the Feb. 21, 1976 rape of an 11-year-old Philadelphia girl.

1976

Nov. 4, 2013
Bailey, an inmate at the State Correctional Institution at Laurel Highlands in Somerset County, Pennsylvania, dies of natural causes.

2013

Nov. 16, 2021
The Rev. Harold Boyd Harrington, Gretchen's father, dies at the age of 94. He leaves behind his wife, Ena, three surviving daughters, and two grandchildren.

2021

This timeline details key dates before and after Gretchen Harrington's kidnapping and murder. *Nicholas Mancini.*

Mrs. Hannig's husband was not home when the murder occurred, but the children—two young sons and two teenaged daughters—were, according to the newspaper.

The Hannig's house was located on what, at the time of the murder, was known as the Hannig farm. It had been occupied by members of the family for at least fifty years and eventually became surrounded by houses that are now part of the Foxcroft neighborhood. A real estate listing notes the home's construction date as 1754.

Lieutenant Mankin was one of the first officers to arrive at the scene of the crime, much like he was when Gretchen's body was found. They would be two crimes he could never shake. Mankin was bent over the body of Mary Hannig when she mumbled information about the men who attacked her, he told the *Daily Times*. She died a short time later at nearby Haverford Hospital.

Several hundred interviews were conducted, but Mary Hannig's killer or killers went unpunished. "I can't begin to tell you the number of leads we pursued," Mankin said.

6

A PRIME SUSPECT

Shortly after Gretchen's disappearance and then grisly murder, authorities began focusing much of their attention on Richard Bailey, a convicted sex offender who had a history of committing violent crimes against young girls. Until this book, Bailey, who died in prison, has never been publicly connected to the case, nor has he ever been formally named as a suspect by police. Bailey is only alluded to in some Facebook posts and web amateur sleuthing websites. But recent interviews with current and former Marple police officers and old police reports in the Harrington case file, including a police interview with a man who placed Bailey near Gretchen on Lawrence Road that fateful morning, all point to the convict, now dead, as a likely culprit in the little girl's death.

Sarah Myers, Ann Myers's daughter and Gretchen's niece, said she was told of Bailey's role as a suspect and that she, like her mother, visited the Marple Police Station hoping to find out more about the crime and Bailey himself. The file on Gretchen's case contains mugshots of a smiling Bailey in a rust-colored shirt and allusions to his truck and himself being at the scene. But it does little to shed light on who this man was other than a criminal who was doing time for sexually assaulting young girls and leaving them for dead.

One thing was clear: Bailey was one of Delaware County's own. He didn't stray far from home in his life or in his crimes. Bailey was a 1964 graduate of Sun Valley High School in Aston, Pennsylvania, a Delaware County town not far from Broomall. His yearbook shows a clean cut, wavy-brown-haired boy in suit and tie. He sported a mischievous grin on his face. He listed his

RICHARD E. BAILEY
120 W. Forestview Rd.
Academic   "Beetle"
Football 2, 3, 4; Student Council 2.

Richard E. Bailey's senior portrait. Bailey graduated from Sun Valley High School in 1964. *Sun Valley High School yearbook.*

nickname as "Beetle" in the yearbook. The young Bailey served on the student council and played football for three years, according to his yearbook entry.

But school apparently wasn't his strong suit. He finished 285th in his graduating class of 287, a fact recounted in a June 1992 *Philadelphia Inquirer* story about inmates at the State Correctional Institution–Graterford earning degrees while behind bars. Bailey was the first Graterford inmate to earn a bachelor's degree in 1987, and he later earned a master's degree in counseling from Liberty University in Lynchburg, Virginia, which was founded by Reverend Jerry Falwell. "Now I'm going to try for my doctorate," said Bailey, who, at the time, had served seventeen years of a twenty-six-year-long stretch for kidnapping, rape and aggravated assault, according to the *Philadelphia Inquirer.* "I'd like to get out and do some counseling."

Bailey had served in the U.S. Army during the Vietnam War, completing advanced infantry training at Fort Dix. He spent time at several addresses in Delaware County, including spots in the towns of Parkside, Drexel Hill and Secane.

Newspaper accounts show Bailey got in trouble with the law not long after high school. He was charged with kidnapping and raping a nine-year-old girl in Springfield on February 26, 1973, according to newspaper accounts. Additional charges in the case included indecent assault, corrupting the morals of a minor, aggravated assault and battery and assault to kill. He was accused of abducting the girl from her home, assaulting her in his car and releasing her, barefoot, in Southwest Philadelphia. Bailey, at the time, was twenty-six, married and working for a finance company, according to court records. But that wasn't his first arrest. Springfield police had arrested Bailey on similar charges in another case in October 1971. He was sentenced to a term of probation, which ended a few days after he was charged in the Springfield case, according to media reports.

Both Bailey and Ena Harrington worked at the Curtis 1000 building in the Lawrence Park Industrial Center but not at the same time, according to police reports. Curtis 1000 is a direct marketing and communications company.

Bailey later pleaded guilty in May 1976 to raping an eleven-year-old Philadelphia girl on February 21, 1976. He was sentenced to twenty-six to fifty-two years in prison on June 15, 1976, by Philadelphia Court of Common Pleas judge Lisa Richette, who noted she felt a duty to send Bailey "away from society for at least twenty-six years," according to media reports.

On February 25, 1976—days after Bailey pleaded guilty in the Philadelphia case—then–Delaware County district attorney Frank T. Hazel subpoenaed Bailey's psychiatric evaluation and treatment records from 1973 through 1976. A November 1, 1973 letter that was sent to Delaware County Common Pleas Court judge Francis J. Catania by a psychiatric consultant, Dr. John K. Fong, after Bailey pleaded guilty in the Springfield case recounted Bailey describing the kidnappings and sexual assaults of two young girls but denying he was sexually attracted to children. He also denied any sexual issues with his wife or any abnormal sexual behavior. The doctor diagnosed Bailey with sexual deviation and pedophilia in a passive-aggressive personality. "It would seem that during periods when this patient is under a great deal of stress at work where his image of himself becomes lessened, he bolsters his ego strength by relating sexually to children," wrote Dr. John K. Fong, who examined Bailey.

At the time of the Harrington kidnapping, Bailey was employed as a maintenance worker at the Park Lane East apartment complex on Garrett Road in Upper Darby. Documents show that on the day of the crime, sometime before noon, Bailey was at a tractor business on Sproul Road in Broomall, about a mile from where Gretchen disappeared, dropping off and picking up lawn equipment. The manager noted that Bailey was not the usual person from Park Lane to do those things and that he "seemed to be in a hurry," documents state.

Bailey had access to a blue 1970 Chevrolet pickup truck that belonged to the apartment complex. On March 4, 1976, the truck was taken to the crime lab for examination, and a dried weed typical of those found in the area where Gretchen's body was found was recovered, documents state.

A friend of Bailey's told police that in the days after Gretchen's body was discovered, Bailey "was wondering how much evidence the police would need to catch whoever it was that did this," documents state. The friend told police that Bailey also described injuries the girl suffered.

Police worked hard to find links between Bailey and Gretchen's disappearance, but there wasn't any physical evidence. However, they did find a witness who seemed to place Bailey at the scene. The woman who called the *Delaware County Daily Times* in December 1975 to say she witnessed the girl's abduction by two men never came forward again with more information about the crime. But there was also a man who approached police with information about seeing Gretchen on Lawrence Road near a green pickup truck on August 15, 1975, the day she disappeared. But at the time, he did not say he could describe or identify the driver.

Police, nearly two years later, questioned that man, Karl Henry Williams, a twenty-seven-year-old parolee who was in Broomall the day Gretchen was abducted. It was the third time they questioned him at length about what he knew about the crime and that day. He was given a polygraph test during the second interview. State Trooper Malcom Murphy and Special Investigator Paul Schneider with the Delaware County District Attorney's Office conducted the September 13, 1977 interview with Williams.

Williams told Murphy and Schneider that he was driving on Lawrence Road toward West Chester Pike around the time of Gretchen's disappearance when he saw a truck race past him and then pull onto the shoulder of the road. He said he saw a girl looking at the truck and the driver. Williams described the girl as having blondish hair and pigtails and said she was wearing blue shorts and a striped blouse. Williams said he did not see the girl get into the truck.

Williams said during that 1977 interview that he could not identify the driver. But he acknowledged that during a prior interview at the state police barracks in Middletown, Pennsylvania, he identified Bailey as the person he believed was the driver after he was shown photographs of about twelve people—including Bailey.

Williams said he believed he had seen Bailey before and after Gretchen's disappearance at the Barclay Square Shopping Center in a bar on Long Lane and at the Sixty-Ninth Street Terminal, all in Upper Darby, Pennsylvania. Williams lived in Upper Darby, which is just across the Philadelphia city line, at the time. Williams said he saw Bailey once after investigators showed him the photographs, when the two were in the Philadelphia Detention Center. Williams said he recognized Bailey, but the two didn't speak.

Williams said he was given a polygraph test at Philadelphia Police Department Headquarters. The interview does not indicate whether he passed. Williams said he was asked numerous times during that test whether he saw the little girl get in the truck. He insisted that he didn't. He told Murphy and Schneider that the officers administering the polygraph told him he lied when he said he didn't see her get in the truck.

When asked why he came forward with the information on the day she was abducted, Williams said he heard about "the preacher daughter's" disappearance from a little boy. Williams had already stopped on the road because of the heavy police and fire presence spurred on by the search for Gretchen. "So, I pulled over and went up to a cop, and I said this little girl you're looking for, what does she look like?" Williams is quoted as saying in the police interview. Williams said he gave police the description of Gretchen, showed them where he saw the truck and said that the truck's tire had left an indent that was still there. He said the police officer took his name and number and said someone would get in touch.

That someone was Marple police Lieutenant Richard Mankin, who was becoming heavily invested in finding Gretchen's killer. Williams said Mankin came to his house and asked him whether he would take a polygraph test. He said he took it and that he was told he passed. Williams said Mankin asked him similar questions to those asked on the polygraph test. But he added one more. "Only I think he asked me if I did it," Williams said in the transcript of the interview with state police.

Williams said he did not tell the police officer on Lawrence Road that day and later Mankin that he witnessed Bailey on Lawrence Road that day he saw Gretchen. He did not give a description of Bailey. He only mentioned the girl and the truck. When asked why he withheld that information, Williams, in the 1977 interview, said he worried the disclosure of identifying Bailey's face would not bode well for him since he was on parole. "I didn't want to get involved really," he said in the transcript. "I was just out of prison myself, you know. I didn't even want to stop, you know, but I stopped."

Williams told police that he didn't fear being named a suspect because he didn't have similar crimes in his background. He feared he could lose his job if his employer found out he was on parole. "It's just that I figured I was just coming out of prison, and I didn't want people bugging me, you know, coming where I work, because where I work, they didn't know I was on parole and just out of prison," Williams told police.

Trooper Murphy queried, "But you did see the driver that day?"

"I seen his face, yeah," Williams responded.

When asked how well he could see Bailey as the truck passed him on Lawrence Road, Williams responded, "I could see his whole face—left side, anyway—when he passed, and his head and his hair," he said.

Police asked whether Williams had ever been to Ridley Creek State Park, the site where Gretchen was likely killed and then discarded before or after the crime. He said yes to both. Police then asked him whether he saw Bailey or his truck in the state park either time. He said no. State Police Trooper Murphy ended the interview at that point.

Williams died on August 6, 2001, at the age of fifty-one.

In January 2006, Marple Township police received a phone call from a Pennsylvania state trooper who had been assigned to investigate the Harrington case. He told a detective about statements that Bailey and Bailey's attorney had made that implied an admission of guilt in the Harrington case, according to case files. The trooper said he interviewed Bailey in prison and that Bailey told him, "If I killed this girl, I must have been sick." The trooper later recounted a conversation with Bailey's attorney, during which the attorney said, "I heard that you were speaking with my client," and then stating a form of "offer" to the effect of: "can a concurrent sentence [to the Philadelphia case] be agreed upon if he [Bailey] pleads guilty to this case?"

The next morning, the trooper spoke to District Attorney Hazel, after which it was decided not to pursue the plea and to continue seeking additional forensic evidence. According to the trooper, there was no additional evidence, the case files state. Hazel later became a judge in Delaware County before retiring in December 2011.

Lieutenant Sean Hannigan, a current Marple police officer, took another look at the case in 2015 and came away with the feeling that there wasn't anything that "jumped out at me. Nothing to bring the case to a close." He looked closely at Bailey and couldn't recall how the man's name surfaced to investigators at the time. "I don't know if he stood out," he added. "I don't recall what made Bailey's name be the popular one."

Barry Williams took a fresh look at the case while serving as a Marple Township police detective in the early 2000s. *Marple Township Police Department.*

But retired Marple Township police detective Barry Williams had a different take when he revisited the case in 2006. "Detective Williams was very determined that Bailey was the guy," Chief Graeff said. Williams was twelve when Gretchen was kidnapped and murdered. His father was a Marple Township police officer when the crime occurred. He talked about picking up the case nearly thirty years later and why Bailey stood out to investigators. "You're leaning toward [Bailey], and people who worked the case before me, the Pennsylvania State Police investigators who I spoke to briefly, they were up in age also, they all indicated their gut was telling them that as well, and they interacted with this guy," Williams said.

Bailey was incarcerated at the state correctional institution at Laurel Highlands in Somerset County, Pennsylvania, when he died of natural causes at a hospital on November 4, 2013, according to the Pennsylvania Department of Corrections. He was sixty-six.

For some retired Marple police officers, the death of the prime suspect in the Harrington case came far too soon. Williams, who was a police officer in Marple Township from 1985 to 2018, said:

> *Unfortunately, I think the guy that died in prison a few years ago* [Bailey] *probably got away with it. The indicators were there—the time, location, space, opportunity was all there—but as far as forensically…if we had the tools we have today, maybe we'd have something. It just wasn't there at that time.*
>
> *We couldn't come to a connection when I looked at the case in '06 to come up with a finalization with the family, the district attorney's office, to maybe offer a deathbed type of scenario where you go out to this guy and interview him, give him another shot, to see if he wants to say something, where maybe it's just for closure's sake. But it never worked out.*
>
> *There was a lot of hearsay, but I still wanted to go out there and take a shot. It just never came to fruition. We couldn't come to an agreement. We never got a definitive answer on which way we were going, then he passes on.*

Larry Gerrity, a retired Marple police detective who worked with Williams, said he still wishes he had one more chance to interview Bailey. "It got too late," he said in an interview. "I always had a fantasy about solving it."

For Gerrity, it became a personal crusade. His life has been linked to the tragedy since he was a teenager. His ex-wife, Jodi Keiser Gerrity, is Dawn Keiser Watson's sister, Gretchen's childhood friend in Lawrence Park. He met Keiser Gerrity while working at the Broomall Kmart store when they were both teens. It was then that she told him her friend had been murdered. He saw the sadness it caused Keiser Gerrity and her sister. Gerrity then went on to become a park ranger at Ridley Creek State Park, and the staff there talked incessantly of the murder. It was then that he discovered the exact spot where the young girl's body had been found.

After joining the Marple Police force, he worked on the cold case, yet another connection to his ex-wife's friend. Now living in Northeast

Pennsylvania, Gerrity said he coincidentally had at one time lived "up the road" from Gretchen's mother and youngest sister. "It's weird. It's been with me my whole life—since I was fifteen," Gerrity said. "I wish I could have done something about it but never got the chance."

Gerrity still feels badly for Reverend Harrington's suffering. He read many interviews in which Reverend Harrington spoke of the pain of losing a daughter. "I can totally see her father sending her up the hill, waving," he said. "He took it hard." Gerrity added, "It's such a shame Gretchen's dad was kind of a suspect....He was the last one with her. The dad is always a suspect. I don't think there's any evidence at all though."

Gerrity said many signs pointed to Bailey, but the evidence was never enough. "By the time I got involved with it, they were looking at Richard Bailey," he said. "We even talked about trying again—we knew he was on his deathbed." Gerrity said Bailey "Mirandaed up," the nickname for using the "right to remain silent" as specified in the Miranda warning that is mandated to be read to all those arrested. The district attorney's office refused detectives' requests to speak to Bailey as he neared death, Gerrity recalled.

But Gerrity said he was told by police that Bailey did say at some point, "It sounds like me, but I don't remember that." when asked at one point whether he kidnapped and killed Gretchen. "I also believe it was him," he said. "'It sounds like me but I don't remember that.' In the police world, that's a confession."

7

A GRIM DISCOVERY

The leaves were just beginning to change at Ridley Creek State Park on an early October afternoon in 2021. Bright yellow and emerging orange leaves comingled with summer's lush foliage in the sprawling park in Pennsylvania's populous Delaware County. The park, dissected by Ridley Creek, sits just sixteen miles from the Philadelphia city line. The park's wooded and winding trails seemed unchanged, though they are probably more overgrown and forested since Gretchen Harrington's body was discovered there on October 14, 1975—almost two months to the day after she disappeared. A visitor on a recent fall day couldn't help but notice how desolate and quiet the 2,606-acre park seemed despite being surrounded by busy roads. Only a few cars dotted the parking lot on a quiet Monday.

Finding the area where Gretchen's body was found has never been easy. To this day, some people still trek to the wooded area of Sandy Flash Drive, a curvy road that loops around the park, to find the spot. Ridley Creek State Park's mystique as the last place Gretchen was likely alive remains for those who are old enough to remember or pass on the story.

In the Marple police case file, that tragic spot is crudely marked with an ink oval on an aging visitor map of the park—a popular place for hiking, family picnics, fishing and camping. The place where she was found— about one and a half miles from West Chester Pike, a main thoroughfare in Philadelphia's suburbs—remains wooded and remote. It requires effort for anyone to go off the main road and into the brush.

Investigators gather along the location where Gretchen Harrington's body was discovered in Ridley Creek State Park on October 14, 1975. *Marple Township Police Department.*

The discovery of Gretchen's body in a state park meant the case immediately drew in the Pennsylvania State Police. Marple Township police suddenly found that their missing persons case had turned into a kidnapping and murder case. Marple police handled the bulk of the kidnapping investigation, while state police focused on the murder in their jurisdiction.

A Marple Township police report from October 14, 1975, said that dispatcher Sheila Bobb called the township police to notify them that Pennsylvania State Police had found human remains in the park and that their presence was requested at the scene. The remains were discovered "some distance" off Sandy Flash Drive at about 4:45 p.m. by a navy seaman, Andrew Louis Van Dyke Jr., who said he visited the park frequently to hike. According to the report, the remains were "skeletonized." Clothing that was found in a neat pile by the remains was tentatively identified as belonging to Gretchen. Detective Richard Mankin told the *Daily Times* two years after the discovery that he still vividly recalled the horror of that discovery. "I remember clearly seeing her," he said.

Pennsylvania State Police interviewed Van Dyke Jr. about the grisly discovery that day, police reports show. Van Dyke worked as a guard at the

This page: The sign at the entrance to Ridley Creek State Park and the approximate location where Gretchen's body was discovered. These photographs were taken in 2022. *Joanna Sullivan*.

The exact location where a jogger discovered Gretchen Harrington's body. *Marple Township Police Department.*

Philadelphia Naval Base. He was not identified at the time the body was found. His name was only disclosed in reports from police interviews that were conducted with him after he said he stumbled upon Gretchen's body. Van Dyke was read his Miranda rights, which law enforcement officers must recite to protect individuals' constitutional rights in custody, before an interview with State Trooper William C. Bandholz, according to a police report.

In the interview, Van Dyke said he arrived at the park at 3:30 p.m. He said he parked his car in the lot for Ridley Creek State Park's Colonial Farm. Also known as the Colonial Pennsylvania Plantation, the historic site and its farmhouse recreates farm life in the region during the period between 1760 and 1790. Van Dyke, an Illinois resident, said he quickly crossed the road, went up the hill to a nearby picnic grove and crossed Sandy Flash Drive to a path he had trekked before. "I was only on the path a short time when I found the body," the twenty-four-year-old told the state trooper in a transcript of the interview.

Trooper Bandholz then asked Van Dyke when he was last on the path where the body was found. Van Dyke said he had been there in the middle of June that year. "If the body would have been there before, would you have seen it?" Bandholz asked. "Yes, I have been on that path three or four times and always travel the same way," he said. He added that he had been coming to Ridley Creek State Park since December 1974 and knew the park very well. He first found it on a Pennsylvania map. He said he was an active traveler who had "been all over" Pennsylvania, New Jersey, New York, Delaware, Ohio, Maryland and North Carolina.

When asked whether he was aware or had read anything about Gretchen's disappearance or other missing girls in Delaware County, Van Dyke simply said "no," according to the transcript. He told the trooper that he never saw anyone on the path during his visits, only soda cans. When asked whether he "associated with any other persons at the park—either employees or travelers—Van Dyke said no. Van Dyke also told police he never took anyone with him to traverse the park's trails. "No, I don't have any girlfriends, and none of the other guys like to do that," he said.

One question in the October 14 transcript centered on Van Dyke stumbling upon Gretchen's remains. He was questioned whether he moved or touched the body in any way. "When I first saw it, I thought it was the body of an animal," he told the trooper. "I looked closely and saw what I thought was fingernails. I lifted one finger with a stick to be sure. When I was sure it was a finger, I went directly to find a park ranger." He said he thought there might be another body at the site, so he kicked at the mound and prodded it with a stick. But he said he thought better of it and decided against it.

When asked whether there was anything he would like to add to this statement, Van Dyke added a simple, "No."

The *County Leader* newspaper reported that the area where the body was found was "thick with knee-high weeds and tall grass, as well as a number of small trees and bushes."

Detective Mankin believed that the killer turned west on West Chester Pike after abducting Gretchen and drove about eight miles to Ridley Creek State Park. "It would have been possible for the killer to drive a vehicle to where her body was found," a secluded area in the park about one mile below West Chester Pike, Mankin told *Delaware County Daily Times* reporter John Roman in a 1988 interview. Police said the body was "lying atop the grass but would not have been visible from any distance because of the undergrowth."

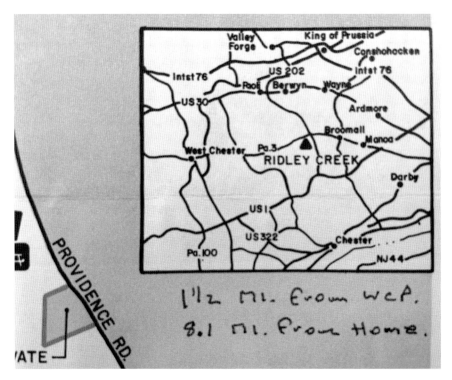

A map showing the location of Ridley Creek State Park, with a handwritten notation indicating that Gretchen was found 1.5 miles from West Chester Pike and 8.1 miles from her home. *Marple Township Police.*

Pennsylvania State Police notified the Harrington family about the remains being found. Ena and Reverend Harrington were escorted in a police vehicle to police headquarters, where they identified the clothing as Gretchen's at 9:12 p.m. "There is absolutely no doubt it was her clothing," Reverend Harrington told the *County Leader* afterward.

At 11:35 p.m., Dr. Halbert E. Fillenger Jr., a forensic pathologist in the Philadelphia Medical Examiner's Office, conducted an autopsy of the remains and positively identified the skeleton as Gretchen's. In his report, he determined that the cause of death was homicide and said that the "skeletonization" of the remains was almost "complete." Gretchen was identified by her teeth, a hair barrette and her clothing. The clothing had been sewn by her mother, Ena.

The copy of Dr. Fillenger's report that was provided for this book was redacted, so it did not include the details of the homicide. But news reports at the time widely reported that the little girl's head had been severely

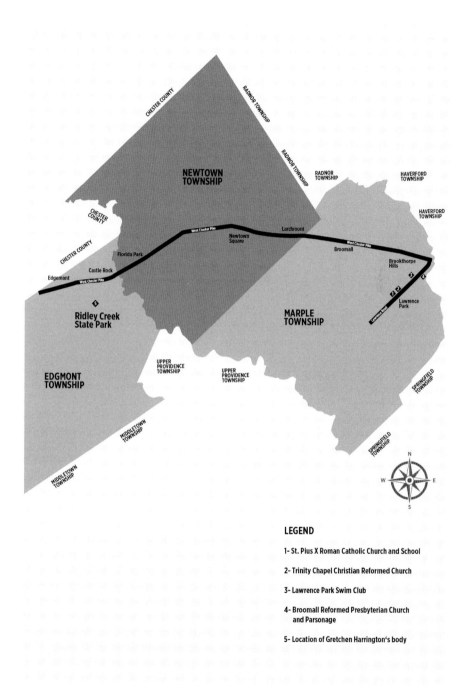

This map shows the distance between where Gretchen disappeared and where her body was found. *Nicholas Mancini*.

Investigators comb the remote location in Ridley Creek State Park where Gretchen Harrington's body was discovered on October 14, 1975. *Marple Township Police Department.*

battered and that she was most likely sexually assaulted. A spokesman for the Delaware County Coroner's Office told the media at the time that death resulted from "two or more severe blows to the head." "We assume she was sexually assaulted," Trooper Malcolm Murphy told the *Delaware County Daily Times*. "There's no other purpose in killing a child."

Lieutenant John McKenna of the Pennsylvania State Police told the *County Leader* that Gretchen was apparently taken to the park and killed there. The decomposition of the body made an autopsy difficult, but police said they were almost certain that the body had been there since August 15, the day Gretchen disappeared. Trooper Murphy, in a *Delaware County Daily Times* interview, said he believed Gretchen, who was last seen at 9:20 a.m. on August 15, 1975, was dead by noon that day.

"We had an idea it would end like this, but all along, we had looked for a miracle," Reverend Harrington told the *County Leader* in an October 15 story. He added that the discovery meant "the loss of all hope" for the family. He acknowledged that there was some relief for the family "in the finality of Gretchen's death," though it was "tragic relief."

Ena Harrington sat down with a reporter in 1988 and revisited that October day. "You never really give up that hope," she said then. "Finding her body ends all that speculation."

Ann Myers, Gretchen's older sister, remembers that all hope dissipated on that long-ago Tuesday. "My parents gave Zoe and me a choice as to whether we wanted to go to school the next day," she said. "For me, that was the end of childhood and an acknowledgement of that end by my parents." She remembers that she realized she and Zoe "could now make important decisions."

"Zoe and I rarely agreed on anything back then, but as I recall it, we discussed it and decided to go," she said. "We knew going would be bad and thought that staying home would be worse. "We were in dread of the circus," she said of the return to Delaware County Christian School the next day. "'Might as well get it over with,' we thought. I understand that I may have come off as cold or uncaring to my classmates. I was too numb to care. After all, they were still children."

Gretchen's friend, Dawn Keiser Watson, recalls her mother walking into her room that day. Her mom told her, "They found her bones. She was dead." "It was sad," Watson added. "I remember crying a lot, and I remember being really scared."

"No one had ever said she had been raped," added Jodi Gerrity. "They just told us someone did something bad to her.…Then life went on."

Life indeed went on for most children, but it was never quite the same for many. The children who might have remembered that day are now adults, and for some of them, they also said they felt the little girl's death meant an end to their own childhood innocence. For some kids, Ridley Creek State Park is forever linked to the crime and seems an unwelcoming, almost ominous place. "I was always afraid to go to Ridley Creek State Park," said Jodi Gerrity, Dawn Watson's sister. Dawn, however, doesn't feel the same way about the state park. "I do enjoy the park," she admits. "My mom would bring us. I think she didn't want us to be afraid of stuff. It has nothing to do with the park. It has to do with bad people." But Dawn said she has never pursued finding the spot where Gretchen likely drew her last breath. "I never saw where they found her," she said. "I don't think I'd want to.'

But Jodi and her ex-husband, Larry Gerrity, say the spot was well-known among those who worked and frequented the park. Larry Gerrity's job as a Ridley Creek State Park ranger would have enabled him to live on the park property in the 1980s. But Jodi said she adamantly refused. She said Larry's coworkers discussed Gretchen's case frequently and could identify the spot where she was found.

Ridley Creek State Park remains a draw for locals and tourists alike, an oasis of sorts amid suburban sprawl and traffic. School groups, families and outdoor enthusiasts still flock there. Carolyn Blanck, who worked as a trail guide at Ridley Creek State Park in the summer of 1975, recalled accompanying a group on horseback when she saw a tree with Gretchen's name carved into it. "I had a group out, and I see this tree up the hill with 'Gretchen' carved into it," she recalled. "It was new. It wasn't a carving that had been in that tree [for a long time]." She then told her father, who got a couple of horses and surveyed the area. Gretchen's body was found not long after that.

There were others who came forward after Gretchen's body was found. They told police about what they considered strange or suspicious sightings in Ridley Creek State Park before and after the grisly discovery. A sixteen-year-old girl from nearby Newtown Square, Pennsylvania, told Lieutenant Mankin that on October 5, 1975—nine days before Gretchen's body was discovered—that she saw a "dirty-looking" man standing in Ridley Creek State Park near where the body was found. She found it "odd." She described the man as being thirty years old, five feet, nine inches tall with short black hair, "apparently of Italian descent," wearing jeans, a light blue shirt and no shoes.

Two other teenage girls reported to Mankin on October 16, two days after Gretchen was found, that during the last week of August 1975—they didn't remember the exact day—a man on that same hill started toward them while hitting one hand into another. They moved away and lost sight of him. But then he showed up again, and the girls quickly went to their car. The man, whom they described as being white, thirty-five to forty years old, with dirty blond hair and wearing a rust-colored shirt and blue cutoffs, came up to their car and apologized for scaring them.

Another suspicious sighting at Ridley Creek State Park wasn't reported to Mankin until June 30, 1976. The woman's manager claimed the woman had reported it the year before, but there was no record of her discussion. Mankin interviewed Sarah "Sally" Worthington, an employee at the Broomall Two Guys, a department store that is now long out of business but was then located near the busy West Chester Pike. Worthington, according to a police report, told Mankin that she went to Ridley Creek State Park on a Sunday morning in late August or early September in 1975 to do some artwork. She was about a half-mile north of where Gretchen's body was subsequently found when a young man in his early twenties came out of a wooded area and just sat in the parking lot in his dark blue Cadillac. Worthington said she stayed in her car, waiting for him to leave. When he didn't, she left the park. She said the man, who had dark brown wavy hair and wire-rimmed sunglasses, followed her in his car. She couldn't shake the man, despite taking a circuitous route around Newtown Square. He finally continued on his way after she pulled into a gas station. She made a sketch of the man for Mankin.

The sightings of men lingering in the park and reports of indecent exposure nearby or attempted kidnappings of children in the subsequent years were never linked to the Harrington crime.

Gretchen's body wouldn't be the last found in the park.

On December 8, 2012, Pennsylvania State Police identified the body of Teresa Mastracola in Ridley Creek State Park. She had been missing since December 2, 2012. In that case, police didn't suspect foul play, according to a story in the *Times Herald*, a suburban Philadelphia newspaper. Mastracola was "an avid hiker and biker who frequented Ridley Creek State Park," according to the article.

Then in January 2016, hikers who were walking in a wooded area along a trail in Ridley Creek State Park discovered the body of a woman who was believed to be between twenty-five and forty years old and white, the *Daily Times* reported. She was fully clothed, wearing cold weather attire, and was approximately between five feet, three inches, and five feet, ten inches tall. Police reported at the time that they believed she had been dead since 2014. The Pennsylvania State Police Criminal Investigation Assessment Unit and the Florida Institute of Forensic Anthropology and Applied Science, University of South Florida developed a facial reconstruction of the unidentified female. The Pennsylvania State Police reached out to the public to help identify the woman.

In 2018, the *Daily Times* again reported that police were seeking help to identify the woman. "Three notable rings were found with the unknown female, including a gold Irish Claddagh ring, a gold initial ring bearing the initial 'C' and a gold diamond ring," the story said. The woman had been wearing Gloria Vanderbilt jeans, a blue winter jacket and size 9 black Totes boots. Investigators found a green plaid blanket, a navy-blue canvas bag, a Route 66 black backpack, a size 9 pair of gray and pink Skechers sneakers, a box cutter and two empty pill bottles near the body.

The woman became known as the Ridley Creek State Park "Jane Doe," and so far, she has never been identified. Investigators believe that no one reported her missing. Speculation about who she was and why she was in

Ridley Creek State Park continues on the internet, another sad mystery forever linked to an otherwise beautiful green space.

Meanwhile, the mention of the park in fall on a recent visit managed to trigger a good memory for Gretchen's sister Ann. "Sometimes, I remember little things about Gretchen," Myers said. "This fall, the goldenrod was everywhere. It's so beautiful and yet makes people sneeze. I don't remember how old Gretchen was, but one year, she gathered a bunch of goldenrod to give to my mother and broke out in hives from it." It's hard not to recall Ann's words when one learns that goldenrod is frequently found in Ridley Creek State Park.

8

THE END OF A "GOLDEN, SUBURBAN CHILDHOOD"

The query on the "Growing Up Broomall" Facebook page, a site with 4,500 members, was lighthearted. It asked the group to name things they remember from their childhood. The answers to the question span a few years, as new members joined and shared their memories.

The Original Thunderbird Steakhouse, a Broomall staple still going strong after sixty-six years, made the list, along with Marple Newtown High School's annual Spring Spectacular Carnival, local pediatrician Dr. Plotkin and "the blind guy who walked up and down Lawrence Road."

"I spent my childhood near the Broomall Little-League field on Foxcroft Road. Great memories of Marple Swim Club, Betsy Parker's penny candy, Presbyterian church strawberry festival and so many friendships. Sadly, it ended when my parents divorced and my dad left. I'll cherish those Broomall years forever," said one group member.

Pamela Jordan posted in the group:

> It's so hard to move on from a place I have such great memories of. My family lived there from 1962 to 1992. They were one of the first families to build in Lawrence Park. We lived on Farnsworth Drive, and it was the best street to grow up on—lots of kids in the neighborhood to play with, then, later on, hang out with. All the families knew each other by name and helped people out.
>
> If I could go back to this, 100 percent, I would in a heartbeat.

But then there was this post from Eileen Gold on August 6, 2011: "I know we have been putting many 'fun' memories, but I have a sad one, and I've been thinking about her lately. I grew up in Lawrence Court Apartments. Our friend Gretchen lived in the church next to our apartments. Late '70s, she was kidnapped, and the outcome was terrible. Rest in peace." After she was contacted through Facebook, Eileen declined to be interviewed for this book. But her comment in 2011 set off a string of comments about Gretchen's death and what it meant to other Broomall residents who were children at the time.

The comments that followed Eileen's post show how this crime remains seared in many people's minds. They can't seem to shake thoughts of Gretchen's loss nearly five decades later.

"I have thought about that so many times. RIP Gretchen," Tara-Leigh Haines Tarantola wrote.

"Gretchen Harrington…I was twelve when she disappeared. I will never forget that day. I remember being at Lawrence Park Swim Club that morning, and we were wondering why the helicopter kept circling the area. I heard the news later that day. I still think about that from time to time, and to this day, it breaks my heart," wrote Laurence J. Miller.

"I don't think any of us ever forgot about it. There was an earlier thread about it, too. First time I ever remember seeing my mother cry," said Tracey Borio Davis.

"You searched for Gretchen Herrington and were forbidden to leave the house for a bit of time—but which seemed like forever. It was never the same for me after that happened, and it still haunts me," Karen M. recalled.

"I vividly remember being so scared when she went missing. I didn't know her, but she lived close enough to make it real to me. I think about her a lot. Every time since then when I went up Lawrence Road. Haunting," added Cory Ilene Solar.

"Every time I think of Trinity Chapel, I think of Gretchen Harrington. Sad," wrote Marilyn Benedict in a thread about the church.

Beth Fleischer wrote, "My life changed drastically the day Gretchen disappeared, and I was no longer outside without supervision at all. I didn't understand then, but I do now."

"It is so weird what sticks with you from childhood. For years, all I remembered was a girl named Gretchen being found in Ridley Creek State Park, and thought I had misremembered somehow, as my parents didn't remember it. I was seven. It stayed with me all these years," wrote Stephanie Lisa.

"I remember the police stopping cars on Lawrence Road to hand out pamphlets about her disappearance. Never forgot that," wrote Lisa Rosenblatt Kaplan.

And with time—and fading memories and newspaper clippings—comes misinformation, as well.

"Yeah, I still think of that every time I see a pick-up [truck]. Wasn't it finally revealed more recently that she actually ran away or was abducted by her own parents or something like that?" Dave Kitabjian asked. One "Growing Up Broomall" member quickly quashed that thinking with a simple, "Dave, no."

That response came from Richard "Dick" Mankin, the Marple police detective who tried for years to solve the case. Mankin posted several times on Facebook threads about Gretchen's death. "Still think of her now and then," he wrote in one thread. Mankin was one of several police officers, spanning decades, who regretted not being able to close the case. His son, Chuck, who has also taken part in "Growing Up in Broomall" chats about Gretchen and said his childhood was altered dramatically after her death. "I know that suddenly, even though it was summer and I was used to playing outside all day and checking in occasionally for lunch, it was different," Chuck Mankin recalled. "At eight, I had the run of the neighborhood, mainly because I lived in a safe town with wonderful neighbors who all knew and cared about each other." He continued, "Gretchen walking that short distance to the church was something we all did back then. Suddenly I wasn't allowed to go very far; suddenly I had to tell where I was going if I was leaving the yard. Little did I know that my parents were scared to death that I'd be next."

Those who were kids back then shared similar stories about their sudden loss of freedom. Their parents said they feared the killer was still on the loose in Broomall. "Everything seemed to be safe, so you didn't worry about things like this," Mankin said.

After Gretchen disappeared, "any car that came into the parking lot of the church, my daughter would come in and say, 'Somebody's in the parking lot,'" said Margie Zandstra, the wife of Reverend Zandstra of Trinity Chapel. "I'd run over and say, 'What are you doing here?'"

"It changed my life, too," Mrs. Zandstra said. "For years, I'd worry about my kids walking alone and not coming home for school on time and that kind of thing."

The Zandstras had arrived at Trinity Chapel from Flanders, New Jersey, in 1969 and stayed until 1976, when they moved with their three daughters to Dallas, Texas. "It was an OK place to live," said Mrs. Zandstra, who grew up in Westfield, New Jersey, and Middletown, near Harrisburg, Pennsylvania, and now lives with her husband outside of Atlanta. "Philadelphia was very familiar to me, but it was not a place I wanted to stay, so after we had been there seven years, we were eager to move on to Texas, a new place, new church and new people."

Shortly after Gretchen vanished, parents approached the Marple Newtown School Board seeking more protection for their kids who were walking to elementary school, according to a story in the *Delaware County Daily Times*. Judy Fingerhood, a parent of a Worrall Elementary School student, called on the board to either get more crossing guards or find some way to get the children to school safely. Another parent, Ronald Brownstein, referenced the disappearance of Gretchen, Wendy Eaton and Debra Jean Delozier in demanding more action from the board. "These children have disappeared in the last few months in Delaware County," he said during a board meeting. "I feel there's a concern by all parents whether they're walking two blocks or eight blocks."

Suggestions to increase busing to school weren't embraced by the board. It wasn't unusual for kids to walk distances just under a mile at the time. Many kids walked unsupervised to elementary and junior high school. The *Delaware County Daily Times* reported that Board President Henry Clay told the parents that he shared their concerns but that Marple Newtown already bused more students on a "liberal scale" than the minimum Pennsylvania requirements. He said there was pressure from "other sides to cut down on busing." Robert Gauntlett, assistant to the superintendent, said he was working with Marple police superintendent Daniel Hennessey to determine if more crossing guards were necessary in the area.

Eventually, the public clamor for more safeguards for their children died down. But the community was never quite the same again. Once they were grown with kids of their own, Gretchen's contemporaries became wary parents themselves. Julie Sealander Higgs grew up in Havertown, just across the Darby Creek from Broomall and within walking distance of Gretchen's home, when the little girl disappeared. Higgs, who was eleven years old in the summer of 1975, recalled:

> *Life was quiet in our small town—we rode our bikes everywhere and played for hours outside in the local creek and explored the woods. It was a time when there was no 24/7 news on the TV or cellphones. There was perhaps an hour of TV news a night and the local newspapers. We had limited exposure to bad news around the country or world.*

So, the kidnapping and murder of Gretchen Harrington was a huge deal—it was such an anomaly to our safe, suburban life. I hadn't thought about this case in decades, but when it was mentioned recently, I remembered Gretchen's name with crystal clarity, and memories instantly came back.

Higgs said that her mother would no longer let her walk alone to the local Manoa Shopping Center about a half-mile away from her home. "My mom was a calm and stable person, not given to becoming overly worried; however, I can't help but think that Gretchen's case made her and other parents more cautious about their kids roaming freely the way we used to," she said, adding, "That sad case took some of the idyllic edge off our golden, suburban childhood."

As a third grader at the Alice Grim School in Newtown Township, Beth Forman Rodinelli was captivated by the case, clipping newspaper articles from the *County Leader*, the area's dominant weekly newspaper at that time. Her mother eventually made her throw out the clippings, she said. "It was so unsettling to me, knowing that a girl my age—that that could happen to her," Rodinelli remembered. "Every time my parents would go to Pathmark, I would always look at the house and the church and just wonder what happened. How could she go missing? The horror just stayed with me." Rodinelli said she has never forgotten what happened to Gretchen and that it made her more conscious of the safety of her own children, even though she enjoyed roaming freely in her neighborhood and in the adjacent woods when she was young. "Even before someone brought it up on Facebook, I always thought about it," she said.

Jamie Famiglio recently walked along Darby Creek, near the Harrington's former home in Broomall, with his seven-year-old daughter. Famiglio, who was thirteen at the time Gretchen was kidnapped, said the case still upsets him. He said it's even worse now that he has a daughter close to Gretchen's age. "Every time I drive up that hill, which is a lot, I think about that kid on the shoulder of the road," said Famiglio, who now lives in nearby Ardmore on Philadelphia's Main Line.

Famiglio grew up in Broomall and worked at his law firm there for thirty-three years. He moved the law firm to Media three years ago after buying a building there. But he returns to Broomall often from his Ardmore home. His daughter loves walking next to the creek to find things. On that recent hike with his own little girl, he noticed that the family who is now living in the Harrington home had toys in the backyard and a trampoline. He couldn't help but think of the little girl who once played in that backyard. "It still affects me," he said. "I wish there had been justice for that kid."

For Dawn Keiser Watson, Gretchen's friend, losing Gretchen also meant the end of attending church or Bible school at Trinity Chapel. "I never went back to church again until I was nineteen," she said, adding that she then became a Catholic. "I was afraid to go to church for fear I would get kidnapped. I assumed walking to church, you could die." She remembers a pastor from the Trinity Chapel coming to visit her to try to convince her family to return to its fold.

Her fear hasn't subsided when it comes to her own kids. "I have trouble letting them go," she said. "I have trouble letting them walk everywhere."

But as hard as it was on the kids, especially those who knew Gretchen, Dawn Keiser Watson thinks it affected her parents even more. Her mother never left her or her sister Jodi alone anymore. Dawn Keiser Watson said she would call if they went to a friend's apartment nearby.

"Nobody knew who it was," she said of the killer. "It could have been someone from our apartment buildings. You weren't allowed out after dark anymore. We didn't play in the courtyard anymore. Everything just kind of stopped."

Keiser Watson's sister Jodi Keiser Gerrity remembers that she and her sister were never allowed to take public transit or trains afterward. "If we went somewhere, my mom drove us," she said. "If we were going to a friend's house, Mom would meet them. My mom would say I would walk away with the devil himself. She really had to watch me."

But Keiser Gerrity doesn't blame her mom for being overprotective. She raised her kids the same way. Former Marple police officer Larry Gerrity, her ex-husband, remembers when their daughter snuck off to Philadelphia. Keiser Gerrity picked her up and was extremely upset and brought up Gretchen's abduction. Their daughter had had enough of hearing about the crime: "I'm not Gretchen," she told her mom. She yelled about always hearing, "Gretchen this. Gretchen that."

Keiser Gerrity remembers that Gretchen's parents were very protective even before their daughter was killed. Gretchen's father came to meet her family before Keiser Watson's eighth birthday party, the day before Gretchen's abduction. "They were a very protective family," she said. "The parents were very cautious with them."

Gretchen's sister Ann Myers said she became a nervous parent and often worried when her kids were out of her sight. Her daughter Sarah Myers recalls her mom's reaction when she didn't come home on time as a teenager. "I remember running around in my neighborhood and not coming home soon enough," she said. "She was distraught and panicked and calling every person."

David Schmid, a professor who focuses on pop culture and crime, said the fact that so many kids and parents—not just the Harringtons and their close friends—were affected by Gretchen's case isn't unusual. The anxiety over one's child being abducted or murdered by a stranger became more prevalent in the late '70s and '80s as cases became more publicized and law enforcement focused on stranger abductions or what became known as "stranger danger."

It's hard to forget the missing children who were featured on milk cartons in the 1980s. Advertisements featured kids who were either abducted by a parent or a stranger. The photographs sometimes showed the expected age progression of the child. Among the kids who were featured was Etan Patz, a six-year-old who disappeared on the way to his school bus stop on May 25, 1979, in Manhattan. The little boy asked his parents if he could walk by himself for the first time. It turned out to be his last.

Patz's case became a national fixation. National Missing Children's Day is held each year on May 25 to commemorate the day he vanished. The Patz case was finally solved decades later and ended with the conviction of Pedro Hernandez, a former bodega stock clerk who confessed to luring the little boy into a basement and murdering him. Hernandez was sentenced to twenty-five years to life in prison in 2017 after a jury trial.

Two years after Etan disappeared, the kidnapping and murder of Adam Walsh also grabbed headlines. It became known as the child abduction that changed America. Six-year-old Adam disappeared in 1981 while shopping with his mom at a Sears in Hollywood, Florida. Sixteen days later, two fishermen found Adam's severed head in a Florida canal.

The case became the subject of a television movie, *Adam*, and turned his father, John Walsh, into a crusading TV star. His first show, *America's Most Wanted*, re-created crimes and urged the audience to help find the perpetrator. Walsh, who continues to advocate for victims' rights, was responsible for the capture of more than one thousand criminals. His latest show, CNN's *The Hunt with John Walsh*, highlights cases of fugitives and expands the search for them internationally. Walsh's crusading ways ushered in an era in which missing and murdered children became the top thing on everyone's mind. But Walsh was never able to bring his own son's killer to justice.

Convicted serial killer Ottis Elwood Toole confessed to Adam's murder twice but was never charged or convicted of the crime. He also recanted his confession and offered investigators differing accounts of the murder, including grisly details of cannibalizing the boy's body. Toole, at one point, blamed notorious serial killer Jeffrey Dahmer, who killed and dismembered seventeen young men and boys in Milwaukee between 1978 and 1991, for Adam's killing. Dahmer himself was murdered by prison inmates. Dahmer denied any involvement in the Walsh killing, despite two witnesses who claim they recognized Dahmer as a man they saw at the mall the day Adam disappeared after he became famous.

Investigators found blood on the carpet of Toole's white Cadillac in 1983, but it wasn't possible at that time to determine whether the blood was Adam's. When that technology to test the blood became available in 1994, the carpet had already disappeared, according to a *New York Times* report.

Toole died in prison in 1996 of liver failure. He had been sentenced to death for killing George Sonnenberg, sixty-four, then indicted in the death of Ada Johnson, nineteen. Toole had also pled guilty to an additional four murders. Florida police declared the Walsh case officially closed in 2008 and named Toole as the killer. No new evidence had surfaced when they made that determination, but Toole's niece had told John Walsh that her uncle had made a deathbed confession to killing Adam, the *New York Post* reported on December 17, 2008.

"Who could take a six-year-old and murder and decapitate him? Who?" John Walsh asked reporters in 2008, according to the *New York Post*. "We needed to know. We needed to know. And today we know.…The not knowing has been a torture. But that journey's over." The blame that was placed on Toole posthumously continues to be debated to this day.

To show how, somehow, the killers of this era had odd connections to each other: Toole also had a connection to the killer Henry Lee Lucas. The pair, both drifters, were apparently friends and lovers, according to news reports. Lucas, as Marple police chief Brandon Graeff said, was, at one point, considered a suspect in Gretchen Harrington's death.

Both the Patz and Walsh cases and others like them prompted child advocates and lawmakers to demand that what was perceived as the growing missing children problem be addressed. John and Revé Walsh, reeling from their son Adam's death, and other child advocates created the National Center for Missing and Exploited Children, a nonprofit national clearinghouse and reporting center for issues related to the recovery and prevention of child victimization. The Alexandria, Virginia organization serves as a resource for law enforcement agencies that are working on cases of missing and exploited children. The nonprofit organization also provides technical assistance to locate abductors and recover missing children.

The outrage over missing and murdered children also led to the 1984 Missing Children's Assistance Act and the demand for an account of just how many children were being affected. The legislation mandated that the U.S. Department of Justice study the phenomenon of missing children. The first of several such reports, known as the "Missing, Abducted, Runaway, and Thrownaway Children in America," came out in 1990 and attempted to compile the number of crimes against U.S. children younger than eighteen in 1988. The first report found that as many as 4,600 children were abducted by non-family members that year and that more than 100,000 kids were targets of attempted kidnappings, mostly by passing motorists.

What surprised many from this study was the number of children—more than 350,000—who were abducted by family members. These cases highlighted often contentious divorces and resulting custody battles. The study also shed light on the huge number of runaways in the country each year. The number totaled about 450,000. If anything, these studies—and those that followed—should have eased some concerns about the likelihood of being abducted, let alone killed, by a stranger. "People feel much more anxious about being a victim from stranger," said Schmid, an author and professor. "You don't want to dismiss that fear and anxiety all together. On the other hand, I never want to lose sight—crimes like stranger killings have always been very, very rare."

Just how rare are these crimes? The FBI reported that, on average, fewer than 350 people under the age of twenty-one had been abducted by strangers in the nation per year between 2010 and 2017. From 2010 to 2017, this number ranged from a low of 303 in 2016 to a high of 384 in 2011.

The National Center for Missing and Exploited Children broke down the cases of missing children in 2020 by category and whether they were active or resolved. The vast majority of missing children, 27,072, were runaways. Family abductions of children totaled 1,396. "Nonfamily abductions" totaled 79, of which 9 cases were listed as active.

The nonprofit expanded its reach in the late 1990s with the help of a private donation. It created the CyberTipline to offer members of the public the chance to report incidents of suspected child sexual exploitation. The center said since its inception, the CyberTipline has received millions of reports concerning crimes against children. The National Center for Missing and Exploited Children also provides mental health support to families dealing with the trauma of not knowing where their child is or, in the worst-case scenario, discovering that they are dead.

Such help and the attention that is now generated for missing children's cases came too late for the Harringtons or the Eatons. Ann Myers said the family was pretty much left to deal with it themselves.

Few people knew of their case outside of the Philadelphia area, and there is no evidence that either case came under scrutiny by the FBI, despite their parents' pleas for help and a resolution from federal agents. The only information about the cases that remains can be found in old news stories, which are often difficult to access because of their age. These victims' names, so well-known in their own tight-knit communities, are not known to the outside world.

The cases of Gretchen and Wendy, however, continue to generate much speculation online, including among amateur sleuths who try to figure out what happened. Too often, the people who have turned true crime into a hobby seem to forget that there were real people involved, despite the years that have passed. That was obvious in one thread on the "You Know You Grew Up in Media, Pa." Facebook page. Wendy Eaton's sister Nancy Eaton addressed the speculation and chatter about her long-lost sister:

> Wendy is my sister, and she was never found. It drives me crazy the stuff that is said about my sister; please, if you have a question, ask me. Unfortunately, I really have no answers. Just to set the record straight: we had tons of family and friends who, for years, helped us try to find her—searched the creeks, abandoned houses, woods, the FBI, psychics, you name it. We were very thankful for all the support we got over the years, but not having a resolution is hard. Nice to know she is not forgotten; she was a kind and thoughtful soul, and I miss her very much.

9

AN OPEN CASE AFTER NEARLY FIFTY YEARS

"My attitude is very simple: I want to see whoever did it brought to justice. We think that justice ought to prevail." Reverend Harrington uttered these words to *Delaware County Daily Times* reporter John Roman in an April 4, 1988 interview.

Harrington died on November 16, 2021, without seeing Gretchen's killer brought to justice. The death of the longtime pastor, husband and father of four devoted daughters and two grandchildren came nearly five decades after the death of his beloved Gretchen. As the years passed, he didn't really expect a resolution. He said as much in that long-ago interview. Though, at the time, he was encouraged when he was told of an arrest of a man in a then-thirty-seven-year-old murder and molestation of an eight-year-old Chester, Pennsylvania girl at a carnival. "We're not living in anticipation the case is going to be solved," he said then.

For the Harringtons and many parents whose child has been kidnapped or murdered, sometimes, there is no resolution. They find a way to live on—some as activists, others retreating to a quiet life. Others struggle for years, perhaps never quite coming to terms with tragedy.

Gretchen's case remains a cold case despite numerous attempts by various generations of officers to solve it. Though some Marple police officers feel like convict Richard Bailey was the murderer, others aren't quite sure he did it. Bailey, who was in jail for raping young girls, died without a confession or a denial. The Pennsylvania State Police refused to comment on former police officers' claims that Richard Bailey was likely

Gretchen's killer, nor would the state police disclose whether DNA is being used to tie Bailey to the evidence found at the scene of the crime. The only mention of DNA testing came in handwritten notes made in 2006 by Detective Barry Williams, a Marple police officer who took another look at the case. In handwritten notes detailing the timeline of Gretchen's murder, he wrote in parentheses, "(Any DNA on soda can or cig [*sic*] butt found in area?)"

DNA and genealogy tracking are being used to find killers and rapists and clear convicts routinely these days. Police, in 2022, finally identified the killer of Marise Chivarella, a nine-year-old girl who was murdered and left in a coal refuse pit in Hazleton, Pennsylvania, in March 1964.

Marise left her house to walk to school and was last seen alive around 8:10 a.m., according to a CNN report. Her body was then discovered in the pit with all her belongings after 1:00 p.m. Police said she had been sexually assaulted. Pennsylvania State Police's use of DNA—used by a team that continued to pursue leads in the case—identified James Paul Forte, who died in 1980, as Marise's murderer in a February 10, 2022 news conference.

In a CNN report, Marise's siblings, who stood by police at the announcement, described Marise as a quiet, sweet girl who had aspirations of becoming a nun. She also enjoyed playing the organ. "We have so many precious memories of Marise. At the same time, our family will always feel the emptiness and the sorrow of her absence," said Carmen Marie Radtke, Marise's sister, during the news conference.

CNN quoted Pennsylvania State Police corporal Mark Baron as saying that the Chivarella case was the fourth-oldest cold case to be solved in the country using genetic genealogy and the oldest in the state of Pennsylvania.

Meanwhile, police in Arizona identified the remains of a four-year-old girl, dubbed "Little Miss Nobody," after more than sixty years in March 2022. She was found in the Arizona desert in 1960. The Yavapai County Sheriff's Office said DNA technology was used to identify Sharon Lee Gallegos, who was snatched from the alley behind her grandmother's backyard in Alamogordo, New Mexico, while playing with two other kids, according to an ABC News report.

The case in Arizona was stone cold until 2015, when the National Center for Exploited and Missing Children offered to help with the exhumation of the girl's remains for DNA extraction and testing. "In 1960, people had no idea that DNA would even be a technology," Sheriff David Rhodes said in the news conference. "They wouldn't even know what to call it. It didn't exist. But somehow, some way, they did enough investigation to preserve, to document, to memorialize—all the things that needed to occur so that someday we could get to this point."

DNA could possibly bring closure to one of the most sensationalized cases of child murder. The killer of Jon Benet Ramsey, the six-year-old Colorado girl who was murdered in her own home in 1996, remains unknown. Her father, brother and now long-deceased mother faced scrutiny for the crime despite there being no evidence that implicated them. Police in Boulder, Colorado, on December 22, 2021, issued a statement that said they were still searching for the little girl's killer twenty-five years later.

The Colorado Bureau of Investigation said it has updated more than 750 reference samples in the case using current DNA technology. "That DNA is checked regularly for any new matches," police said. "As the department continues to use new technology to enhance the investigation, it is actively reviewing genetic DNA testing processes to see if those can be applied to this case moving forward," the Colorado agency said in a statement. While the DNA found at the crime scene hasn't caught the killer, it helped clear the name of Jon Benet's parents, Patsy and John Ramsey, and her brother, Burke, who was nine at the time, of the crime in 2006. The family had long been seen as suspects in the case by both the police and the public.

Cold cases continue to be solved through the use of DNA evidence. In fact, the use of DNA and convicted DNA databases has grown significantly since the first U.S. DNA database was started in 1989. All states require at least some convicted offenders to provide a DNA sample to be collected for DNA profiling.

Genetic genealogy—the use of DNA to discover one's origins and potential relatives—is now helping law enforcement catch criminals decades after they committed their crimes. Police are using the genealogy craze to connect the dots in cases where they have the DNA of a suspect who isn't in a DNA database. Instead, police find relatives, often distant, who can connect them to the suspected killer or rapist.

The practice helped nab the Golden State Killer, a serial rapist, burglar and former police officer who is suspected of killing at least thirteen people, raping fifty and committing 120 burglaries in California between 1974 and 1986. Investigators traced crime scene DNA that had been stored to a distant relative of the killer. The relative had been innocently trying to fill out their family tree by taking a saliva test for a genealogy website.

Joseph James DeAngelo, a former policeman, was arrested in 2018 on eight counts of murder and pleaded guilty to his crimes two years later. Prosecutors agreed to take the death penalty off the table in exchange for his plea. DeAngelo was sentenced to eleven consecutive life sentences. Investigators had linked DeAngelo to the crimes after trailing him and capturing "discarded DNA" from items he left behind. The pieces all fell together in the DeAngelo investigation. That's not always the case when you're dealing with decades passing between the crime and the investigation.

Peter Feeney and John McCarthy, who prosecuted the Lyons' sisters' killer in Maryland, said time makes solving a crime, let alone convicting someone for it, nearly impossible. "Criminal cases are not like fine wines," McCarthy said. "The cork spoils, and you lose the whole bottle." He said, too often, investigators will go down "rabbit holes" when trying to find a killer. "And ultimately, you're going to get to a person you need to talk with, and they're going to be dead," he said.

Then there's the issue of manpower and cost in investigating a cold case. "Ultimately, it's a resource issue," Feeney said. "It's just this enormous investment to try to solve a case like this."

Feeney and McCarthy said they enlisted the aid of the FBI in creating a profile of the likely offender in the Lyons' case, and they eventually landed on Lloyd Lee Welch. The information helped them learn how to question Welch, whom they described as a "psychopath." For example, they learned that appealing to Welch with pleas to help the Lyons' parents give their daughters a proper Christian burial—something dubbed "the Christian burial speech"—would never work with a psychopath. He wouldn't have sympathy for the parents. Instead, the profile helped police remain calm in dealing with Welch. There was no yelling or screaming. They were able to win him over with some level of trust—and McDonald's cheeseburgers— during the interviews.

McCarthy said he imagines that a profile of Gretchen's suspected killer exists somewhere. No such profile exists in Marple Township police's box of evidence. Then again, there's no evidence of FBI involvement in the case, despite pleas from the Eatons and Harringtons that federal law enforcement get involved in the case.

Graeff, the Marple police chief, said it wasn't unusual in the 1970s for local jurisdictions to go it alone. The FBI and local police didn't talk much, let alone work together on cases. The FBI typically came in if someone was taken or a crime was committed across state lines. "In 1975, it wouldn't even dawn on me to call the FBI," Graeff said. "It's different now for sure." He added, "If the exact same thing happened today, they would be the first call." Graeff said local police can rely on the resources of the FBI in such a case today. He is unaware of whether the Pennsylvania State

Marple Township police chief Brandon Graeff. *Joanna Sullivan.*

Police are attempting to use DNA to find Gretchen's killer or perhaps link the crime to suspect Richard Bailey.

Graeff's candor about the Harrington case stood in stark contrast to the refusal of the Pennsylvania State Police to discuss it at all and the reluctance shown by Delaware County district attorney Jack Stollsteimer to talk about Gretchen's death or the disappearance of Wendy Eaton in Media. When asked about the status of the Harrington case, Stollsteimer said only, "Every unsolved homicide is an open case. There's no statute of limitations on homicide." He added that an open case doesn't mean it is being actively investigated. He acknowledged that "there hasn't been a new lead in forty-six to forty-seven years" in the Harrington case.

Stollsteimer, who grew up in nearby Havertown, was twelve in 1975. He said he had no recollection of Gretchen's case or that of Wendy Eaton's disappearance.

Stollsteimer spoke publicly in May 2021, when Pennsylvania State Police investigators changed Eaton's disappearance case to a homicide and dug on a property, presumably in search of clues or her body. "I believe the state police have done a remarkable job of getting this case to the position where

Delaware County district attorney Jack Stollsteimer. *Jack Stollsteimer.*

we're in right now," Stollsteimer said then. "Where we think we can find some physical evidence on that property."

In a May 2021 story by NBC Philadelphia, Stollsteimer would not confirm whether they were investigating the people who previously lived in the house near the search area in 1975. "We certainly can't talk about individuals or that part of the investigation, but what I can tell you is that property is of interest to us for significant reasons," he said. "There's probably one person out there in your audience who will see this who can probably give us a tip or might be able to help us solve the case," Stollsteimer told NBC10.

But Stollsteimer, who was interviewed again in April 2022, refused to provide any updates on the Eaton case, nearly one year after the digging on the property began. "There's been no updates required up to this point," he said, adding that "we're hopeful all unsolved murders can be solved." He did, however, say state police investigators were working hard to solve the case. "If anybody can solve it, it's going to be these guys," he said. Stollsteimer also declined to discuss Richard Bailey as the suspect in the Harrington case or whether there was any connection to the Eaton case.

But the district attorney was less close-lipped about wanting public exposure on both cases to possibly trigger memories for someone or to create new leads. "There is somebody out there who knows exactly what happened," Stollsteimer said. "There are probably more people who know what happened. It they would come forward, that would be a wonderful thing." He said a book about the Harrington and Eaton cases could prompt someone to think, "It's finally time for me to come forward." "Come forward," he added. "Release the family of this young girl of this purgatory by letting them know what happened."

With every passing year, the pool of people who may have seen or known something diminishes.

Reverend Harrington, in a 1988 interview, said he was convinced there was still someone out there who knew something they weren't sharing. "I've always been persuaded there's somebody who knows something that happened," Reverend Harrington told the *Delaware County Daily Times*'s John Roman in the interview. "Probably the person involved is a relative [of someone who knows something] and simply don't want to expose somebody who's precious to them."

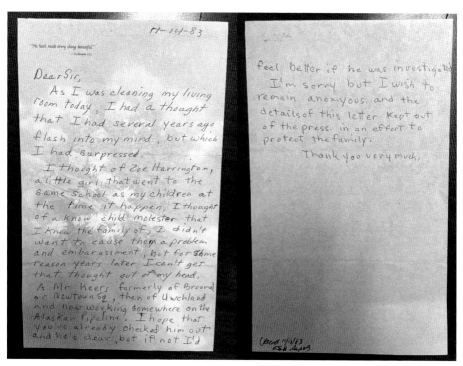

11-14-83

"He hath made every thing beautiful." — Ecclesiastes 3:11

Dear Sir,

As I was cleaning my living room today, I had a thought that I had several years ago flash into my mind, but which I had surpressed.

I thought of Zoe Harrington, a little girl that went to the same school as my children at the time it happen, I thought of a know child molester that I knew the family of, I didn't want to cause them a problem and embarassment, but for some reason years later I can't get that thought out of my head. A Mr. Keers formerly of Broomall or Newtown Sq, then of Uwchland and now working somewhere on the Alaskan Pipeline. I hope that you've already checked him out and he's clear, but if not I'd

feel better if he was investigated. I'm sorry but I wish to remain anonymous. and the details of this letter kept out of the press. in an effort to protect the family.

Thank you very much,

Marple Twp. Police
Springfield & Sproal Rd
Broomall
19008

In November 1983, Lieutenant Richard Mankin received this anonymous handwritten letter in which the writer identifies a potential suspect in the case, "a Mr. Keers, formerly of Broomall or Newtown Square, then of Uwchland, and now working somewhere on the Alaska pipeline." Mankin appealed publicly for the author of the letter to come forward, but police records do not show if the man was located or interviewed. *Mike Mathis.*

The woman who called the *Delaware County Daily Times* but didn't call back is one of those reluctant witnesses. Another was a person who wrote a letter after she said a memory popped into her head as she was cleaning her living room. The letter was delivered to a Marple police detective in November 1983. The person claimed to have children that attended Delaware County Christian School with Gretchen and her sisters Zoe and Harriet (Ann). "I thought of a known child molester that I knew the family of. I didn't want to cause them a problem and embarrassment, but for some years later, I can't get that thought out of my head," she wrote. The woman went on to name a man by last name only who used to live in Broomall and was working "somewhere on the Alaskan Pipeline. "I hope that you already checked him out and he's clear, but if not, I'd feel better if he was investigated," the letter said. The woman went on to apologize for wanting to remain anonymous and said she wanted the details of the letter to be kept out of the press to protect the man's family.

Detectives who were working on the Harrington case made a public appeal to the author of the letter to offer them more details. The person was never heard from again.

Police Chief Graeff said such clues continue to be looked at and talked about in the hopes that perhaps someone may still come forward. "You never know what triggers a bit of information, jostles someone's memory," Graeff said. "You just can never close a case until it's closed."

That lack of closure dogged Detective Richard Mankin in the waning years of his career and into his retirement. "Gretchen's case was a very big deal for our community and, in turn, for him," said his son Chuck Mankin. "I feel like not being able to find who kidnapped and killed her felt like a defeat to him. He was a great cop and a top-notch investigator, too. I know because my brother and I rarely got away with anything"

Reverend Harrington's daughter Ann Myers doesn't hold out hope that the killer will be found. She's still trying to heal from decades of grief and trauma.

Myers and her daughter, Sarah, talked about creating a public memorial for Gretchen somewhere in Delaware County. Myers always felt like she didn't have anywhere to mourn or visit her sister. Gretchen was buried in the Harrington family burial plot in Hetherton, Michigan, Reverend Harrington's hometown. Myers recalls that though they still lived in Broomall, bringing Gretchen's body back to Michigan was a way to avoid the grave becoming a destination for gawkers. Her parents wanted her away from the scene of the crime, she recalled.

But her sister's faraway grave has always meant that there was no place for Myers to visit. It was something that troubled her over the years. She knew that members of the community might want something to remember Gretchen as well. But Myers had a change of heart after her father, Reverend Harrington's November 2021 death. She would finally have a place to pay her respects to her sister—and now her father.

Reverend Harrington, who served in the U.S. Navy in World War II, was buried in Washington Crossing National Cemetery, a cemetery that was opened in 2019 to serve U.S. veterans. The 205-acre burial place is just three miles from the spot where General George Washington famously crossed

The final resting place of Reverend Harold Harrington, who is interred at the Washington Crossing National Cemetery in Upper Makefield, Pennsylvania. *Mike Mathis.*

the Delaware River during the Revolutionary War. The cemetery in scenic Bucks County, Pennsylvania, is only about an hour away from Myers' home in York, Pennsylvania.

Myers said, "I know we spoke about a memorial for Gretchen, but if there were such a thing, my family would not be involved," she said. "We would want something private. My father is interred in Washington Crossing Military Cemetery, and for me, that is now a place I can go to remember my father and also Gretchen."

Myers's anger remains at the still unknown killer, his atrocious act against her sister and the legacy he left her family.

"Accidents are horrible, but it's still something people know how to handle," she said. "If you die any other way, you get some kind of honor. People remember you in a good way."

SHE HATES THAT HER sister's tragic death overshadows the girl herself. "That's what I want for her—to be remembered for being a sweet little girl," Ann said. "She didn't do anything wrong. She had no part in her own demise."

BIBLIOGRAPHY

Bodek, Ralph. *How and Why People Buy Houses: A Study of Subconscious Home Buying Motives*. Philadelphia, PA: Municipal Publications Inc., 1958.

Broomall Fire Company. https://broomallfirecompany.com/.

Burlington County Times

Chester Times/Delaware County Daily Times

Cinema Treasures. http://cinematreasures.org/.

County Leader

Dixon, Mark E. "Ralph Bodek's Lawrence Park Showed Builder's—and Buyer's—Split Personalities." Main Line Today, July 12, 2016. https://mainlinetoday.com/life-style/ralph-bodeks-lawrence-park-showed-builders-and-buyers-split-personalities/.

Lane, Barbara Miller. *Houses for a New World: Builders and Buyers in American Suburbs, 1945–1965*. Princeton, NJ: Princeton University Press, 2015.

Marple Historical Society. http://www.marplehistoricalsociety.org/history.html.

Marple Police. https://www.marplepolice.com.

Marple Township EMS. https://marpleems.com/history/.

Marple Township Police Department files

Mathis, Mike. *Marple and Newtown Townships*. Charleston, SC: Arcadia Publishing, 1998.

News of Delaware County

Pennsylvania Historical and Museum Commission. "Pennsylvania's Historic Suburbs." http://www.phmc.state.pa.us/portal/communities/pa-suburbs/research-tools/primary-research.html.

Philadelphia Bulletin

Philadelphia History Museum. "Museum History." http://www.philadelphia history.org/about/museum-history/.

Philadelphia Inquirer

1696 Thomas Massey House. http://www.thomasmasseyhouse.org/.

ABOUT THE AUTHORS

Mike Mathis has worked in the communications field for more than thirty-five years. He has worked as a publications and video manager for the New Jersey Courts, where he was responsible for the design and content of print and web-based publications and videos. He was also a reporter and editor for several newspapers, including the *Burlington County Times* in Willingboro, New Jersey, where he covered the state and federal criminal and civil courts, major crime, school districts and municipal government. He has been an adjunct professor in the Visual, Performing and Communication Arts Department at Camden County College since January 1995.

A graduate of Villanova University, he is the author of five books published by Arcadia Publishing and is the coauthor of *Cherry Hill: A Brief History*, published by The History Press. He also works as a freelance writer and is a contributor to the *Encyclopedia of New Jersey*, published by Rutgers University Press in 2004, and *State Supreme Courts*, published by the National Center for State Courts in 2013.

A Cherry Hill, New Jersey resident, he is married and has three children and four grandchildren.

Joanna Sullivan has been the editor-in-chief of the *Baltimore Business Journal*, part of the American City Business Journals publications, for more than twenty years. She has also worked as an editor and reporter for the *American Banker* newspaper in Washington, D.C.; the *Annapolis*

Capital in Annapolis, Maryland; and the Hagerstown, Maryland *Herald-Mail*. She's a graduate of the Phillip Merrill College of Journalism at the University of Maryland, College Park. A native of Philadelphia, she lives in Baltimore with her husband, Michael, and son, Maxim.